Our Science

Hiroaki Tanaka

Hiroyuki Yamanishi

Bill Benfield

photographs by
iStockphoto

Unit 1　画像提供：Environment International
Unit 2　「深海未来都市構想 OCEAN SPIRAL」画像提供：清水建設株式会社
Unit 6　画像提供：Science
Unit 15　画像提供：Human Communication Research

Our Science

はじめに

　本書は身近な科学をテーマに、それに関連する最新の研究成果や未来の姿を予見させる技術革新について大学生に分かりやすいような英文で書き下ろしました。主なテーマはテクノロジー、環境、建築、生物、バイオサイエンス、都市計画、行動科学、人体、そして科学倫理と幅広く設定し、理系学部の学生だけでなく、文系学部の学生も興味を持てるような内容にしました。

　本書は中上級総合英語教材として、各ユニットの英文の語数を 550 語から 650 語程度に設定してありますが、辞書に頼ることなく内容理解ができるようにしています。

　本書の特徴は Reading と Writing を 2 つの柱とした構成です。Reading で内容を理解するだけでなく、パラグラフ構造も理解し、それをライティングスキルとして Writing 活動に応用する構成になっています。Reading で扱われた文章をいわばお手本として、それを活用、あるいは応用して自分の英語で書く演習ができます。もう 1 つの本書の特徴は Listening と Speaking に加えて、Active Learning も取り入れて総合的で能動的な学習教材になっている点です。Reading テーマをさらに深めた内容のダイアローグを用いて、聞き取りや会話活動の演習をします。その後、テーマに関連した図表の読み取りをしたり、自分でリサーチした内容をプレゼンテーションしたり、あるいはリサーチを踏まえて自分の意見を述べたりする演習があります。これによって、理解した内容を書いたり、話したりすることで、能動的に理解を深められます。最後に、各 Unit のテーマに関連した最新の研究成果が本文や Active Learning で扱われている点も特徴です。中には *Nature* などのトップジャーナルも含まれていますが、大学生の皆さんに理解しやすいように平易に書き直したり、エッセンスのみを紹介したりしています。興味を持ったテーマがあれば、将来的にその原典を読むなどのチャレンジもしてもらいたいと思っています。

田中 博晃

山西 博之

Bill Benfield

CONTENTS

本書の使い方

Warm Up

　各 Unit のテーマの導入となります。学生のみなさんにとっては身近なテーマもあれば、そうでもないものもあるかと思います。クラスメイトと情報交換したり、インターネットなどでテーマの背景知識を調べたりするなど、自宅で予習をしておくと理解が深まります。本書は身近な話題に関する世界の最新の科学研究の成果を取り扱っています。各 Unit のテーマが、現在の科学技術でどのように進歩しているのか想像力を働かせてください。

Vocabulary

　本文に使用される重要な語句を 10 語ずつ抽出しました。高校で既習の語とそうでない語の両方が含まれます。できるだけ辞書に頼らずに解答し、その後、辞書で意味と発音を確認してください。

Reading Comprehension

　読解問題です。Comprehension Questions A は本文の内容との正誤を判定する TF 問題で、正確な読解力が要求されます。Comprehension Questions B は本文の全体像を理解する問題で、次の Writing 活動につながる設問です。パラグラフ構造を意識しながら解答してください。また辞書を使わずに読むことが理想ですが、自分の語彙力にあわせて適宜使用しても構いません。

Writing

　パラグラフライティングの習得に焦点を当てています。ここでは各 Unit で取り上げるライティングスキルの解説と演習を取り扱います。各スキルは本文でも使われていますので、それを応用して自分の英語で表現する練習をします。また各スキルを応用する際に Unit によっては有用なシグナルワードのリストや演習があります。単に表現を覚えるだけでなく、その使い方も意識して学習してください。

Active Learning

　Listening & Conversation ではモデルダイアローグを使いリスニングとスピーキングの演習をします。各 Unit のテーマに関連あるいは発展した内容について大学生 2 名が議論しています。その音声を聞いて空欄を埋めるディクテーション活動の後、モデルダイアローグで Speaking の練習をしてください。次の Discussion では各 Unit のテーマについて、図表を読み取ったり、自分の意見を述べたりする発展活動です。各 Unit で学習した語彙や表現、ライティングスキルなどを活用しながら解答してください。

UNIT 1

No Car, Happy Life?
Carless Cities in Spain

車のない街はパラダイスかもしれない

I Warm up

Imagine if no vehicles were allowed to enter your home-town. What would your life be like? Share your ideas with your partner.

II Vocabulary

Match each word or phrase with its meaning.

1. automobile _____
2. considerable _____
3. inhabitant _____
4. impose _____
5. measure _____
6. eliminate _____
7. pedestrian _____
8. volume _____
9. restrict _____
10. implement _____

a. 居住者　　b. 方策　　c. 量　　d. 自動車　　e. 歩行者　　f. かなりの
g. 課す　　h. 取り除く　　i. 実行に移す　　j. 制限する

Read the passage and answer the questions.

1 If we compare photographs of cities taken 100 years ago with the same cities today, the most striking difference is the absence of automobiles. All around the world, so much of our current urban environment is dedicated to vehicle traffic and its supporting infrastructure—roads, bridges, tunnels, parking lots, etc.—that
5 it is hard to imagine a city where the needs of people take priority over those of cars. But in Spain, there are two cities that have mounted initiatives to return urban space to their citizens.

2 One of these places is Pontevedra, a city of 84,000 people in the northwest of the country, which has reduced car use by 90 percent in its historic center and by
10 half in the city as a whole. The benefits to the city have been considerable. The number of deaths in traffic accidents has dropped significantly; carbon dioxide emissions are down by almost 70 percent; crime rates have fallen; the center of the city has gained 12,000 new inhabitants; and even though Spain's birthrate is declining, the city's child population has increased by eight percent because of its
15 popularity with young families.

3 Behind the project is Miguel Lores, who has been mayor of Pontevedra since 1999. He has a simple philosophy: owning a car does not give people a right to occupy public space. Whereas other cities have tried to reduce traffic through imposing strict measures such as fees, fines, and legal bans, Lores took a different
20 approach. Pontevedra eliminated all surface parking in the city center. Instead, it provided underground parking lots and more than 1,600 free parking spaces on the edge of the city to discourage people from driving to the center. It has also designed many of its streets as loops, which prevents people from driving through the city. In some areas, sidewalks have been removed entirely as a way to
25 stress that the streets are primarily intended for pedestrians, not cars. In addition, posted around the city are subway-style maps that indicate how long it takes to walk from one place to another.

4 The other Spanish city making efforts to reduce traffic volume is Barcelona. With 1.6 million people, it is considerably larger than Pontevedra and has one of
30 the largest population densities in all of Europe. The city suffers from excessive noise and air pollution caused by vehicle traffic. Studies have established that Barcelona's poor air quality causes several thousand premature deaths every year in the city's metropolitan area.

5 Barcelona's approach to dealing with its traffic problem is to create so-
35 called "superblocks." These are groups of streets where traffic is almost entirely eliminated so that pedestrians can walk, and children can play safely. Traffic

is restricted to roads around the edges of these superblocks. Vehicles are
40 only allowed to enter if drivers are residents of the area or if they are providing services to local businesses, and their speed is limited to
45 10 kilometers per hour.

6 At present, the plan is operating in only a few areas of the city, but if it is fully implemented, it will
50 create 503 superblocks. This would bring a number of important benefits. One study calculates that the city could prevent 667 traffic accidents every year, reduce NO_2* emission levels by 24 percent, and increase the life expectancy of the
55 average Barcelona resident by almost 200 days.

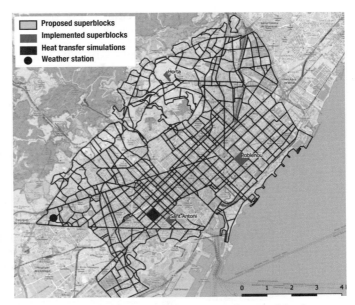

Figure. Barcelona's 503 proposed superblocks.

7 Pontevedra's city planning and Barcelona's Superblocks could be notable examples of a paradigm shift away from the car-centered urban planning model and toward a people-centered approach. Such successful urban planning needs strong leadership with a clear and consistent vision. The vision should also be
60 co-developed with citizens and all other stakeholders such as local businesses. This can ensure that everybody shares ownership and takes responsibility for the success of local initiatives.

NOTES ....

NO_2 二酸化窒素 （呼吸器の病気の原因になる大気汚染物質）

Comprehension Questions A

Choose T if the statement is true or F if it is false.

1. Technological and social developments have resulted in cities that are more convenient for people rather than for vehicles. ⬚T ⬚F
2. In Pontevedra, no cars are allowed to enter the city because all streets are fully pedestrianized. ⬚T ⬚F
3. If a car enters the south of Pontevedra, it cannot simply pass through to leave by the north. ⬚T ⬚F

4. Superblocks are groups of streets where the space formerly occupied by cars is given over to pedestrians. ☐T ☐F

5. Barcelona's superblocks have already saved hundreds of citizens' lives and cut air pollution by a quarter. ☐T ☐F

Comprehension Questions B

The figure below shows the overall organization of the passage. Choose the best answer to fill in the blanks.

Introduction

Paragraph 1: In today's world, most people live in cities built with extensive space and infrastructure for (1.   ). However, two cities in Spain are reimagining their future to be more (2.   ) centric.

Example 1

Paragraph 2: Cars are banned from Pontevedra's city center, creating a model for a pedestrian-friendly city. It brings social and health (3.   ) to its residents.

Paragraph 3: Miguel Lores introduced unique (4.   ) for the pedestrianization of the city such as implementing new traffic and parking plan, and making maps with travel distances and routes for pedestrians.

Body

Example 2

Paragraph 4: Barcelona is plagued by air pollution and noise due to heavy traffic density.

Paragraph 5: Barcelona has created superblocks, which reclaim streets from cars and transform them into (5.   ) public spaces.

Paragraph 6: There will be potentially significant (3.   ) regarding traffic accidents, emission levels and life expectancy if Barcelona's superblock model is fully implemented.

Conclusion

Paragraph 7: For successful people-centered urban planning, every citizen must share ownership and take (6.   ).

(1) _____   (2) _____   (3) _____   (4) _____   (5) _____   (6) _____

a) walkable   b) measures   c) benefits   d) beneficial   e) human
f) responsibility   g) automobiles   h) walk

Ⅳ　Writing

Paragraph Structure and Organization

　論理的な文章は一定の「型」（あるいは作法）に従って書かれます。これは読み手に過度な負担をかけず、伝えたい情報を確実に伝達するためです。型には大きくは文章全体の「構成」（organization）があり、主張を提示する「導入」（introduction）→具体的な例などを示す「本論」（body）→まとめを行う「結論」（conclusion）といった構成が一般的です。各段落の中では、「主題文」（topic sentence）→「支持文」（supporting sentences）→「結論文」（concluding sentence）といった「段落構造」（paragraph structure）が基本の型です。また、これらを読み手にうまく伝えるため、情報整理や交通整理の役割をする「シグナルワード」を用います。

　このセクションでは、まず段落構造を理解した上で（Unit 1 ～ 4）、代表的な文章構成の型を学び（Unit 5 ～ 9）、その後より発展的な型に触れ（Unit 10 ～ 13）、最後に応用的な要約作成の演習を行います（Unit 14・15）。

　段落（パラグラフ）と文章全体（パッセージやエッセイ）の基本的な構成要素を整理したものが以下の図です。

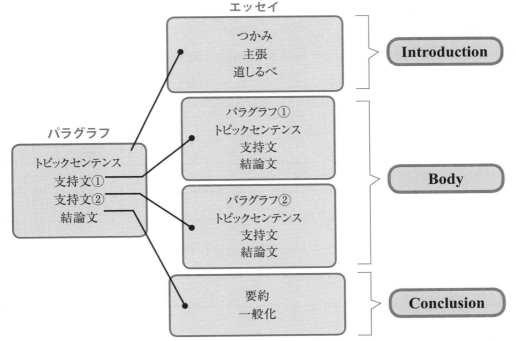

図：パラグラフからエッセイへの展開（川西, 2019 に Introduction、Body、
　　Conclusion の情報を追加）

Active Learning

Listening & Conversation

Listen to the dialogue and fill in the blanks. Then, practice the dialogue with your partner.

A: Look at this statistical analysis on car accidents in Japan. It says
(^{1.}   ) 500 thousand car accidents have been
(^{2.}   ) in Japan every year.

B: That's a huge number!

A: Yes. It means more than one car accident happens every minute.

B: Well, it also says (^{3.}   ) accounted for the largest share of road deaths—nearly 40% of the total.

A: And about 70% of these occur while people are crossing the road.

B: So, we should be more careful when crossing the road.

A: More than half the car accidents happen in (^{4.}   ) areas.

B: I hope the government (^{5.}   ) car use in large cities.

Discussion

Do you think we need a paradigm shift to carless cities? Discuss your ideas with your partner.

....
....
....
....
....
....
....
....
....
....
....
....

UNIT 2

Science Fiction Is Not Fiction: Building Down and Building Underwater

SF が現実に：地下都市や海中都市は実現可能か？

I Warm up

Underground facilities such as subway stations and shopping arcades can be found all over Japan. What do you think is the deepest facility in Japan and how deep is it? Share your ideas with your partner.

II Vocabulary

Match each word or phrase with its meaning.

1. accommodate _____
2. encompass _____
3. exploitation _____
4. dual _____
5. operate _____
6. prohibit _____
7. diameter _____
8. pathway _____
9. quest _____
10. in response to _____

a. 二重の   b. 開発   c. 歩道   d. 収容する   e. 包含する
f. 〜に応えて   g. 探求   h. 直径   i. 禁止する   j. 稼働する

Read the passage and answer the questions.

1 For hundreds of years, when human beings needed more space to accommodate growing populations in towns and cities, we built outward. Urban areas spread to encompass more and more of the surrounding land. In the 19th century, however, progress in constructing buildings using a steel framework and
5 the invention of the elevator enabled us to go upward. Now, there is increasing interest in maximizing our useable space by building downward.

2 Needless to say, building underground is far from a new idea. Beneath our feet as we walk through our cities lie myriad structures, including underground walkways, shopping arcades, utility pipes, subway lines, and emergency shelters.
10 In Tokyo, for example, 282 stations are located underground, the deepest of which is Roppongi Station, lying 42 meters below the surface. But there hasn't been much use of underground space beyond a depth of 50 meters. For the cities of the future, such exploitation of the ground beneath them will continue, but at the same time, is sure to become more adventurous and innovative.

15 **3** One country where underground space is already utilized in an impressively systematic way is Singapore. This is hardly surprising since the tiny city-state faces the dual problem of scarce land and a growing population. At present, Singapore's underground infrastructure operates on three different levels. The first is from one to three meters, with pedestrian links connecting one area to another. Next
20 is the 5-to-50-meter level. This is the location of the Common Service Tunnel, which houses telecom cables, power lines, and water pipes. A little further down are tunnels for trains and other vehicles. On the third level, which lies at a depth of 100 meters and below, is a large-scale ammunition depot*. Finally, at a depth of 150 meters is an enormous oil storage facility. By putting as many services as
25 possible beneath the surface, Singapore is attempting to leave land above ground available for urban development.

4 Elsewhere, there are much more ambitious projects, one of which is planned for Mexico City. Mexico's huge capital needs new infrastructure as well as space for offices, shops, and homes. But not only are there no empty plots available,
30 there are also laws prohibiting the demolition* of historic buildings as well as height regulations that limit new buildings to eight stories. This means the only option is to build downward. In response to this challenge, architects have designed what they call an "earth-scraper," a 65-story inverted pyramid that will descend 300 meters below ground. Once completed, it will contain space for
35 homes, shops, offices, and even a museum. The center of the pyramid will be hollow so that all floors will receive natural light.

5 Another project, which seems almost to have sprung from the pages of a science
40 fiction novel, is the brainchild of Japanese construction company Shimizu
Corporation. Named Ocean Spiral, it is an underwater city
45 of 5,000 people that draws energy from the seabed thousands of meters below. According to an architect's model, the structure will be

Figure. Ocean Spiral.

50 divided into three sections. Just beneath the surface of the sea, there will be a
floating sphere 500 meters in diameter. This will contain businesses, residences,
and hotels. Connected to this will be a 15-km-long spiral pathway, which will lead
to the ocean floor 3 or 4 km below. Here, researchers will investigate methods of
extracting energy resources from the seabed. Scientists at Shimizu estimate that
55 the technology necessary for its construction will be available in 15 years from
now.

6 In its quest for expansion, the human race has always looked for new frontiers
to conquer. Always assuming it is possible, the colonization of Mars or other
planets is likely to lie in the distant future. In the meantime, however, going
60 downward—either on land or at sea—seems to offer exciting possibilities.

NOTES ....

ammunition depot 弾薬庫, **demolition** 破壊

Comprehension Questions A

Choose T if the statement is true or F if it is false.

1. Paragraph 1 suggests that in the 19th century, we erected tall multi-story buildings
   to make the best use of limited land.   T F

2. In Tokyo, it is difficult to construct any facilities beyond a depth of 50 meters.
                                                                            T F

3. Singapore has already moved infrastructure, residential areas, fuel storage, and an
   ammunition depot below ground.   T F

4. An earth-scraper aims to expand Mexico City's residential, commercial, and
   cultural capacity.   T F

5. Ocean Spiral is under construction and due for completion in 15 years from now.
                                                                            T F

Comprehension Questions B

The figure below shows the main points of each paragraph's topic sentence. Choose the best answer to fill in the blanks without looking back at the passage.

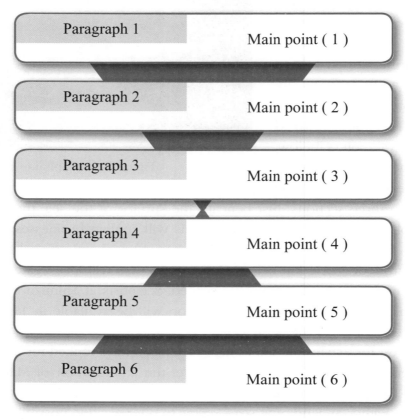

Paragraph 1	Main point (1)
Paragraph 2	Main point (2)
Paragraph 3	Main point (3)
Paragraph 4	Main point (4)
Paragraph 5	Main point (5)
Paragraph 6	Main point (6)

(a) Another project (①) by a Japanese construction company.

(b) Building underground as existing idea.

(c) Far more (②) project for Mexico City.

(d) Exploiting downward as an exciting possibility.

(e) Singapore's systematic (③) of underground space.

(f) Increasing interest in quest for a downward world.

(1) _____   (2) _____   (3) _____   (4) _____   (5) _____   (6) _____

(①   ) (②   ) (③   )

a) devised   b) prohibited   c) ambitious   d) utilization   e) utilize

Ⅳ Writing

Introduction / Topic Sentence

　本 Unit では、文章全体の「導入」(introduction) の段落の役割と、各段落の「主題文」(topic sentence) の役割を確認します。

introduction とは
introduction の役割は文章全体の見通し図の提供です。以下の内容が含まれます。
- 「つかみ」(**hook**)：読み手を引きつける情報や読み手を「置いてけぼり」にしないための前提情報。本 Unit の 1 段落目 For hundreds of years, when human beings needed more space to accommodate growing populations in towns and cities, we built outward. が該当します。
- 「主張」(**thesis statement**)：書き手の意見や文章全体で説明する内容の要点。本 Unit の第 1 段目 Now, there is increasing interest in maximizing our useable space by building downward. が該当します。
- 「道しるべ」(**sign posts**)：単純には、There are three reasons. / I have three reasons. などの文章全体の交通整理や予告情報。実際の文章では、より複雑かつ高度な表現を用いることが望ましいです。また、分量等のバランスから 2 段落に分かれることも多いです。本 Unit では 2 段落目が該当します。

topic sentence とは
topic sentence の役割はそれぞれの段落の「主題」(**main points / main ideas**) を述べることです。主題を含んだ topic sentence は 1 ～ 2 文で構成され、各段落のはじめ、あるいは終わりに置かれることが多いです。

　実際には上記の情報を適宜取捨選択し、読み手にとって興味深く読みやすい文章になるように工夫しましょう。また Unit 1 の図（パラグラフからエッセイへの展開）も参照してください。

Write a paragraph in English giving your opinions about the reading passage in this unit. Pay special attention to the organization, especially to the information that should be included in the introduction and/or the topic sentence. You can use the words and phrases you learned in the passage or comprehension questions.

....

....

....

....

Active Learning

 1-16

Listen to the dialogue and fill in the blanks. Then, practice the dialogue with your partner.

A: Do you know the name of a town where most of the people live underground?

B: No! I can't even imagine it. What's it called?

A: Coober Pedy.

B: I've never heard of it.

A: It's an Australian town 846 km north of Adelaide. Many of Coober Pedy's (1.   ) live underground to (2.   ) the region's intense heat.

B: How hot is it?

A: Temperatures in the town's summer months can (3.   ) 50 ℃. Most of the local population is (4.   ) inside sandstone. The town has a (5.   ) of underground shops, bars, museums, and churches to visit.

B: That's very interesting. I'd like to go there someday.

Discussion

Where would you prefer to live, underground or underwater? Discuss your ideas with your partner.

....

....

....

....

....

....

....

....

....

....

....

UNIT 3
Save Summer Heat for Winter: Air Conditioning Past and Future

夏の暑さを保存して冬の暖房に：エアコンの過去と未来

I Warm up

How many air conditioners are there in the world? Share your ideas with your partner.

II Vocabulary

Match each word or phrase with its meaning.

1. indispensable _____
2. humidity _____
3. adversely _____
4. exposure _____
5. storage _____
6. emission _____
7. sustainably _____
8. molecule _____
9. throw away _____
10. in turn _____

a. 捨てる   b. 貯蔵   c. 不可欠な   d. 持続可能に   e. 湿度   f. 分子
g. 今度は   h. 排出   i. 逆に   j. さらされること

13

Read the passage and answer the questions.

1 For people in developed countries, air conditioning is an indispensable feature of modern life, just like an uninterrupted flow of electricity or running hot and cold water. But making life more comfortable for human beings was not its original purpose. Air conditioning was actually conceived with an industrial
5 application in mind.

2 The first air conditioning system was designed for a color printing factory in New York in the early 20th century. The operators of the business discovered that changes in humidity adversely affected the printing process, resulting in a large number of defective copies that had to be thrown away. To solve the problem,
10 Willis Carrier, an American engineer, designed a system that would regulate temperature and humidity in the company's factory. At first, air conditioning was used mainly in industries such as textiles, printing, and food processing, but in the 1920s, some department stores and movie theaters began to install systems. With the popularity of air conditioning on the increase, the first individual
15 window units were produced in 1932. Currently, there are more than 1.6 billion air conditioning units in use around the world, and the global demand will only increase from now on. It is estimated that the number is expected to be 5.6 billion over the next 30 years.

3 We would be wrong to think, however, that the only role of cooling technology
20 is to provide relief and comfort in hot weather. It also plays a vital part in keeping people safe and healthy. Influenza vaccine, for example, should be stored in a refrigerator or handled at temperatures between 2 and 8 ℃ for any period of time. Using refrigerators to maintain recommended temperatures and protect against other environmental exposure during vaccine storage, transportation,
25 handling, and administration processes is critical in preventing damage to the vaccine. However, according to the WHO, in India, for instance, almost 20 percent of medical products that depend on cold supply chains arrive in an unsatisfactory state because of insufficient cooling. Also, food producers such as farmers and fishermen suffer economically if they are unable to cool their products long
30 enough to get them to market.

4 But, at the same time, cooling poses a risk to the global environment. Increased use of cooling products leads to increased emissions of hydrofluorocarbons* (HFCs). These substances have an effect on global warming 23,000 times greater than that of carbon dioxide (CO_2), which in turn creates greater demand for
35 cooling products. In addition, air conditioning takes heat from the inside and then pumps it straight out into the atmosphere, which makes cities hotter and can

raise night-time temperatures by up to 2 ℃. As a result, people turn up their air conditioning even higher and so we become trapped in a vicious circle.

5 The crucial point, then, is to devise a way to sustainably cool our world

40 without harming the environment. One high-tech solution is being developed by researchers in Sweden. They have been making significant progress in developing a specially designed molecule that can store solar energy for future use. When this molecule is hit by sunlight, it is transformed into an energy-rich molecule. This molecule can then be stored for times when it is needed. It exists in liquid form

45 and can be used in solar energy systems. The energy it contains can be stored for up to 18 years. The researchers have given it the name MOST, which stands for Molecular Solar Thermal Energy Storage*.

6 Coming up with ways to prevent cooling from heating up our world even further will certainly be a challenge, but it is one that is likely to spur even greater

50 creativity and innovation among scientists, inventors, and private companies.

> **NOTES** ···

hydrofluorocarbon 代替フロン, **Molecular Solar Thermal Energy Storage** 分子ソーラー熱エネルギー
貯蔵

Comprehension Questions A

Choose T if the statement is true or F if it is false.

1. Air conditioning applications were invented because of the need to cool air for personal comfort. T | F

2. The worldwide demand for air conditioning is expected to double over the next 30 years. T | F

3. Without cooling technologies, we would not be able to store medicines safely or prevent food from rotting. T | F

4. Ironically, our dependence on air conditioning seems to worsen the original problem. T | F

5. The development of a specially designed molecule enables us to store solar energy from the summer sun for use in winter. T | F

The figure below shows main points of topic sentence and supporting sentences in paragraph 4. Choose the best answer to fill in the blanks.

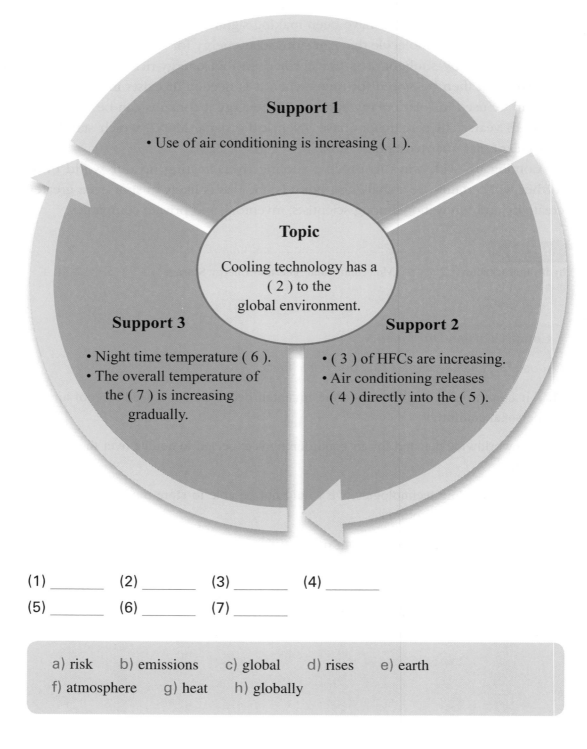

Support 1

• Use of air conditioning is increasing (1).

Topic

Cooling technology has a (2) to the global environment.

Support 3

• Night time temperature (6).
• The overall temperature of the (7) is increasing gradually.

Support 2

• (3) of HFCs are increasing.
• Air conditioning releases (4) directly into the (5).

(1) _____ (2) _____ (3) _____ (4) _____

(5) _____ (6) _____ (7) _____

a) risk   b) emissions   c) global   d) rises   e) earth

f) atmosphere   g) heat   h) globally

Ⅳ Writing

Body / Supporting Sentences

　本 Unit では、文章の中核をなす「本論」（body）の段落の役割と、各段落の「支持文」（supporting sentences）の役割を確認します。

body とは
body の段落の役割は、導入（**Unit 2**）で示された「主張」（thesis statement）をいくつかのサブトピックに分けて、具体的に発展・展開することです。body はサブトピックの数に応じて複数の段落で構成されますが、基本的に 1 つの段落で 1 つの内容を発展・展開します。body には主題文、支持文、結論文が含まれます。結論文が次の段落へのつなぎになる場合は「移行文」（**transitional sentence**）とよびます。

supporting sentences とは
supporting sentences の役割は主題（トピックまたはサブトピック）をサポートする詳細情報を述べることです。supporting sentences は通常複数のセンテンスから構成され、以下の内容が含まれます。
- 「支持詳細」（**supporting details**）：主題をどのようにサポートできるかを的確に表す内容。
- 「エクステンダー」（**extenders**）：指示詳細をさらに発展的に説明する内容。具体例や統計情報、引用情報等を含みます。

なお 1 段落で完結する文章の場合、supporting sentences は、複数段落からなるエッセイやパッセージの body の役割を果たします（Unit 1 の図も参照）。

Write a paragraph in English giving your opinions about the reading passage in this unit. Pay special attention to the organization, especially to the information that should be included in the body and/or the supporting sentences. You can use the words and phrases you learned in the passage or comprehension questions.

....
....
....
....

Active Learning

Listening & Conversation

 1-23

Listen to the dialogue and fill in the blanks. Then, practice the dialogue with your partner.

A: I never knew that using air conditioning has a negative impact on the global environment.

B: Me neither. It needs electricity to run. If electricity comes from fossil fuels, the environmental impact is worse.

A: We should (1.   ) to natural energy like solar energy.

B: But solar energy is weather-dependent. Though solar energy can be (2.   ) during cloudy and rainy days, the efficiency of the system drops.

A: That's right. Solar energy (3.   ) is expensive, too.

B: I heard that Tokyo University has invented heat-storage ceramics. They can store heat energy for a long period and release it on demand.

A: That's a wonderful (4.   ). This technology is similar to the MOST system in Sweden.

B: I hope we can (5.   ) use air conditioning.

Discussion

What are the advantages and disadvantages of MOST? Discuss your ideas with your partner.

....

....

....

....

....

....

....

....

....

....

....

UNIT 4

Are You Ready for Cultured Meat?

シャーレから生まれた培養肉の衝撃：家畜が消える未来

I Warm up

Can you imagine meat that does not come from animals? What is it and where does it come from? Share your ideas with your partner.

II Vocabulary

Match each word or phrase with its meaning.

1. embedded _____   2. dietary _____   3. slaughter _____

4. intriguing _____   5. extract _____   6. synthetic _____

7. unveil _____   8. culture _____   9. authentic _____

10. make the switch _____

a. 本物の   b. 切り替える   c. 培養する   d. 発表する   e. 食事の
f. 埋め込まれた   g. 抽出する   h. 食肉解体する   i. 魅力的な   j. 合成の

Read the passage and answer the questions.

1 What is the best way to reduce our environmental impact on Earth? Most people would probably say using renewable energy, cutting down on flights, or driving an electric vehicle. But according to a recent study on farming published in the journal *Science*, the single most effective solution would be for people to
5 move to a lifestyle which excludes all animal-based foods such as meat, dairy, and eggs—that is, a vegan diet—because feeding the world in this way would be a much more efficient way to use our agricultural resources. It is estimated that meat and dairy products provide just 18 percent of our calories and 37 percent of our protein while they use 83 percent of farmland and produce 60 percent of
10 agriculture's greenhouse gas emissions.

2 However, it is highly unlikely that enough people in the world would be willing to make the switch. For many people, meat consumption is so deeply embedded in their dietary preferences that they will not easily be persuaded to give it up. But there is another potential solution: creating meat in a way that
15 does not involve raising and slaughtering massive numbers of animals. A leading global consultancy firm has recently released a report that says by 2040, most of the meat people consume will not come from slaughtered animals. It will come partly from using plant-based products designed to look and taste like meat. This approach is not new: so-called "vegan meat," usually made from soybeans,
20 wheat gluten*, and vegetables, has been available for several years now. A more intriguing approach is to scientifically "grow" meat in laboratories.

3 The first step in creating such meat is to extract stem cells from muscle tissue. These cells are cultured with nutrients and chemicals that promote growth so that they develop and multiply. After about three weeks, when the stem cells number
25 more than a million, they are put into smaller dishes, where they combine to form small strips of muscle about one centimeter long and a few millimeters wide. When there are enough of these strips, they are combined to form larger pieces of meat.

4 Unfortunately, the kind of meat resulting from this method is unlikely to
30 entice meat lovers because it cannot produce large recognizable chunks of meat, like a steak. Synthetic meat has therefore typically taken the form of processed meat such as ground beef, which can be turned into hamburger steak. In fact, the world's first lab-grown burger was unveiled in London in 2013. It was eaten by two food critics, whose reaction was positive on the whole. However, we
35 should not expect burgers of this kind to appear on menus any time soon: it cost over $300,000 to make and took more than two years to produce. They estimate

that it will take around ten years to develop the mass-production technology required to put the process into practical use.

5 The road to producing cultured meat that would satisfy committed meat eaters is likely to be a long one. But progress so far shows that the potential exists to make a product that is cheaper, healthier, and less damaging to the environment than the meat we currently consume.

NOTES ....

gluten グルテン, **whitish** 白っぽい

Choose T if the statement is true or F if it is false.

1. Vegans do not eat foods that come from animals such as meat and eggs but they do eat yogurt and cheese. ☐T ☐F
2. Paragraph 1 suggests that meat and dairy products cause more environmental harm than vegetable growing. ☐T ☐F
3. In the future, most of the meat people eat will come from conventional meat markets. ☐T ☐F
4. Paragraph 4 implies that the price of a cultured burger left a great deal to be desired. ☐T ☐F

Comprehension Questions B

Read again the conclusion paragraph below that comprises two sentences, and choose its function respectively.

(1) The road to producing cultured meat that would satisfy committed meat eaters is likely to be a long one. (　　)

(2) But progress so far shows that the potential exists to make a product that is cheaper, healthier, and less damaging to the environment than the meat we currently consume. (　　)

(a) supporting detail

(b) paraphrased summary of the passage

(c) generalization of what has been discussed so far

(d) new supporting information to convince the reader more

Ⅳ Writing

Conclusion / Concluding Sentence

　本 Unit では文章のまとめとしての「結論」（conclusion）の段落の役割と、各段落の「結論文」（concluding sentence）の役割を確認します。

conclusion とは
conclusion の段落の役割は、導入と本論の内容をまとめて、文章を終えることです。以下の情報が含まれます。
- 「要約」（**summary**）：主張と本論の各主題の内容を「別の表現」で簡潔にまとめ直すこと。要約については Unit 14 〜 15 も参照。
- 「一般化」（**generalization**）：本論での主張や議論を一般化し、文章を締めること。

concluding sentence とは
concluding sentence の役割は、主題で示された内容を「別の表現」で繰り返し、まとめ直すことです。別の表現で「言い換える」（paraphrase）ことで、読み手は単調な印象を受けにくくなります。それに加えて結論を一般化した内容も含まれることがあります。

conclusion の段落や concluding sentence に含めない方が良い内容
上記の一般化を除いて、これまで述べてない新情報を含めてしまうと、かえって読者を混乱させてしまうので避けましょう。

Write a paragraph in English giving your opinions about the reading passage in this unit. Pay special attention to the organization, especially to the information that should be included in the conclusion and/or the concluding sentence. You can use the words and phrases you learned in the passage or comprehension questions.

....

....

....

....

Active Learning

Listening & Conversation

Listen to the dialogue and fill in the blanks. Then, practice the dialogue with your partner.

A: Have you ever heard of (1.   ) meat?

B: Is it a meat-like (2.   ) made from plants, like vegetarian meat?

A: No, they're different. Vegetarian meat is plant-based, and contains ingredients such as soybean and gluten.

B: I know. Vegetarian meat is already on the (3.   ). Otsuka Foods produces plant-based hams and sausages.

A: Cultured meat is created by more (4.   ) technology, in which meat is produced by in vitro cell culture of animal cells.

B: It sounds like future technology. So, we won't need to (5.   ) cows or pigs on farms if this technology becomes common.

Discussion

Which would you choose, cultured meat or meat from animals? Discuss your ideas with your partner.

....

....

....

....

....

....

....

....

....

....

....

....

....

UNIT 5

Good News: Ozone Hole Is Recovering

オゾンホールは回復していた！？：国際協力の成果

I Warm up

You may know the expression "ozone hole." What is it and how large is it? Share your ideas with your partner.

II Vocabulary

Match each word or phrase with its meaning.

1. ultraviolet _____   2. stratosphere _____   3. atom _____
4. supposition _____   5. coordinated _____   6. depletion _____
7. satellite _____   8. ban _____   9. circulation _____
10. come under threat _____

a. 禁止する   b. 脅威にさらされる   c. 紫外線の   d. 協調的な
e. 仮定   f. 減少   g. 循環   h. 衛星   i. 成層圏   j. 原子

25

Read the passage and answer the questions.

1 Anyone who has experienced a painful case of sunburn knows that we have to be careful not to expose ourselves to excessive amounts of strong sunlight. In extreme cases, ultraviolet (UV) radiation from sunlight can cause skin cancer and cataracts*. Luckily, high up in the stratosphere, we have a filtering mechanism
5 that protects us—a layer of ozone that absorbs a large amount of UV radiation and prevents it from reaching the surface of the planet. Ozone is basically oxygen, but unlike the oxygen we breathe, which is made up of two oxygen atoms (O_2), ozone has three (O_3).

2 This protective ozone barrier came under threat from chemicals known as
10 chlorofluorocarbons* (CFCs). Invented in 1928, these chemicals have been widely used in refrigerators, air conditioners, and aerosol sprays. As their use expanded, especially in developed countries, an increasing amount was released into the atmosphere. In the 1970s, however, scientists theorized that these gases had the potential to damage the ozone layer. These suppositions were confirmed when
15 a so-called "ozone hole" was detected above Antarctica in 1987. Strictly speaking, an ozone hole is not an absence of ozone, but an area where its concentration* is below a certain threshold.

3 In contrast to the current lack of coordinated action on climate change, the international community recognized the danger posed by ozone depletion and
20 took prompt steps to limit the volume of CFC emissions. In 1987, countries around the world came together to sign the Montreal Protocol*, an agreement to regulate the production and consumption of ozone-depleting substances. Naturally, results did not come straight away, and levels of ozone-depleting substances continued to rise until around the year 2000. Since then, though, they have continued to decline
25 slowly.

4 Despite this fall, an ozone hole still forms over Antarctica every year around September or October, and it is still huge. In 2018, data from NASA's observation satellites estimated that it covered 22.9 million square kilometers, or roughly 60 times the size of Japan. However, climate scientists say that chlorine levels in the
30 stratosphere over Antarctica in 2018 were down 11 percent from their peak and that, 20 years ago, the same weather conditions would have created a much larger hole. What is more, the Antarctic ozone hole in 2019 was the smallest observed (16.4 million square kilometers) since 1982. This seems to be evidence that global efforts to tackle the problem are succeeding. Improvements, however, are gradual,
35 and scientists expect that we will have to wait until around 2070 for Antarctic ozone to recover to its 1980 level.

5 Even though efforts to rescue the ozone layer are proceeding broadly according to plan, a recent study published in the journal *Nature* has shown that CFC-11* is not declining as fast as expected despite being banned. Although
40 levels of CFC-11 showed a steady drop between 2002 and 2012, the decline since then has slowed down. Researchers found that the decline of the concentration of CFC-11 in the Southern Hemisphere has been constant but that in the Northern Hemisphere, especially in East Asia, has clearly slowed down since 2012. The researchers suggested a possible and disappointing scenario on the basis of these
45 results. The most likely answer is an increase in unreported CFC-11 emissions, which is inconsistent with the Montreal Protocol agreement. Scientists warned that if the new sources of unreported production are not shut down, it could delay the healing of the ozone layer by a decade.

NOTES ....

cataract 白内障, **chlorofluorocarbon** フロンガス, **concentration** 濃度,
the Montreal Protocol モントリオール議定書, **CFC-11** フロン 11

Comprehension Questions A

Choose T if the statement is true or F if it is false.

1. The ozone layer in the stratosphere shields life on Earth from harmful ultraviolet radiation. ☐T ☐F

2. The ozone hole is technically a "hole" where no ozone is present. ☐T ☐F

3. The Montreal Protocol is a landmark agreement that successfully reduced the global production and consumption of ozone-depleting substances, and had an immediate effect on ozone layer recovery. ☐T ☐F

4. According to paragraph 4, specialists are optimistic about the huge ozone hole observed in 2018. ☐T ☐F

5. According to the last paragraph, it seems someone is producing a banned ozone-depleting chemical again. ☐T ☐F

The chart below shows the time (chronological) order of the events described in the paragraph 2 to 4 of the passage. Choose the best answer to fill in the blanks.

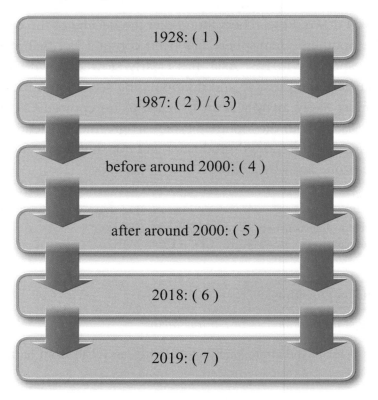

1928: (1)

1987: (2) / (3)

before around 2000: (4)

after around 2000: (5)

2018: (6)

2019: (7)

(a) Ozone-depleting substances decreased slowly.

(b) An ozone-depleted area was first detected.

(c) Countries agreed to sign an international treaty designed to protect the ozone layer.

(d) An artificial chemical, later theorized to be an ozone-depleting substance, was invented.

(e) The smallest ozone hole ever was observed.

(f) Ozone-depleting substances increased.

(g) The ozone hole was still huge, but chlorine levels were down 11 percent from the peak.

(1) _____ (2) _____ (3) _____ (4) _____

(5) _____ (6) _____ (7) _____

Ⅳ Writing

Organization 1 （Time Order）

Unit 5 ～ Unit 9 では代表的な文章構成の型を学びます。

色々な出来事を順を追って整理して説明するには、「**時系列**」（**time order** あるいは **chronological order**）の文章構成が有用です。その場合、読み手が混乱しにくいように「古いものから新しいもの」あるいは「新しいものから古いもの」に並べるのが一般的です。明確に年号や時刻等を用いる方法もありますが、そういった情報が使用できない時には、出来事の順序や前後関係を明示するシグナルワード（Unit 1 参照）を用います。

シグナルワード

first, second, last, next, then, before, after, at the end, in advance, to begin with, at the same time, meanwhile, since then

● Exercise

Put the words and phrases in right order.

(1) 私たちが直面している問題を解決する前に、何がその原因かを探求することが重要である。

(solving, facing, the problems, before, are, we), it is important to explore what is the cause of them.

....

(2) 教授の研究室を訪ねる際、事前にメールで訪問の連絡を入れておく方が良いだろう。

When you visit a professor's lab, it's better to (in, visit, inform, email, the professor, of, your, by) advance.

....

Rewrite paragraph 2 of the passage without using the year of each event but use the time order signal words instead. You can use the words and phrases you learned in the passage or comprehension questions.

....

....

....

....

Active Learning

Listening & Conversation

Listen to the dialogue and fill in the blanks. Then, practice the dialogue with your partner.

A: The recovery of the ozone hole is good news, isn't it?

B: Yes, it really is. I think the Montreal Protocol is one of the most successful world
(1.   ) in history.

A: I agree. In 2018, NASA found the first direct evidence that the ozone hole was
recovering. They used (2.   ) for observation and directly
measured levels of stratospheric chlorine to see whether the international ban on
CFCs was effective.

B: Wow, that's a large-scale survey! But I heard someone is producing
(3.   ) chemicals again.

A: Yes, I'm really concerned about it.

B: A recent article in *Nature Climate Change* proposed CFCs have not only an
(4.   ) effect but also a global warming effect. The article
estimated the far north is heating up twice as fast as the global
(5.   ).

A: I didn't know that! We must severely restrict the use of CFCs.

Discussion

The figure below compares the size of the ozone hole every five years since 1979 (except 1995, when no data was available). What can you tell from the data? Discuss your ideas with your partner.

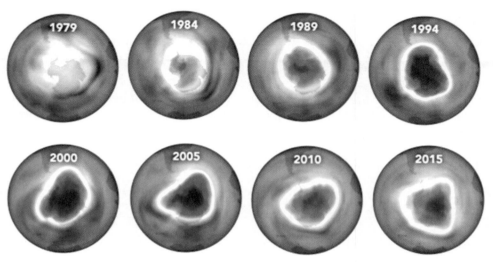

Figure. The size of the ozone hole every five years.

Note. Taken from NASA's earth observatory 2018 and revised by the authors.

UNIT 6

Lost Wallet: Will You Ever Get It Back?

お金が入っているほど落とした財布は返ってくる？

I Warm up

Have you ever lost your wallet? Was it returned to you? Share your experience with your partner.

II Vocabulary

Match each word or phrase with its meaning.

1. probability _____
2. exception _____
3. respectively _____
4. honesty _____
5. reputation _____
6. statistics _____
7. obligation _____
8. shed light on _____
9. find way back _____
10. a great proportion of _____

a. 大多数の　　b. 可能性　　c. 評判　　d. 正直　　e. それぞれ　　f. 統計
g. 例外　　h. 義務　　i. 元の場所にたどり着く　　j. 〜を明らかにする

III Reading Comprehension

Read the passage and answer the questions.

1 You reach for your wallet, but you find that it has gone. In a panic, you realize you must have dropped it somewhere. Has it gone forever, or will some kind person find it and return it to you? A recent research project conducted by universities in the United States and Switzerland attempted to shed light on the
5 probability of a lost wallet finding its way back to its owner. One of the results of the study may come as a surprise.

2 In the three-year experiment, researchers posed as people who had
10 found a wallet on the street. They would take the wallet into a public institution such as a post office or a hotel and hand it to a staff
15 member. They then asked that person to take care of it. Each wallet contained business cards with an email address to allow the
20 "owner" to be contacted directly. Some wallets contained money, and some did not. The value of the money in the wallet was
25 constant—the equivalent of around $13 in local currency. They planted

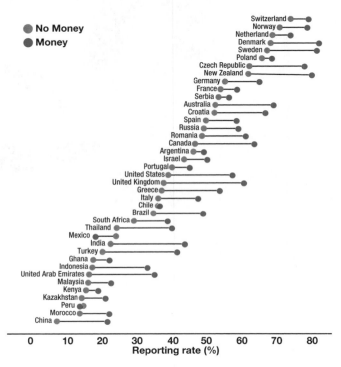

Figure. Share of wallets reported in the No Money and Money conditions by country.

more than 17,000 wallets in 355 cities in 40 countries, covering every continent except Antarctica. In Asia, the countries where the experiment was performed
30 included China, Malaysia, India, and Thailand.

3 The results show that people are less selfish and more altruistic than we might imagine. With the exception of two countries (Peru and Mexico), a greater proportion of people emailed to return wallets containing money than cashless wallets—51 percent and 40 percent, respectively. If we look at a breakdown of
35 the results to find the most honest countries, we see that overall, the top three were Switzerland, Norway, and the Netherlands. As far as the return of wallets

containing money was concerned, Denmark, Sweden, and New Zealand came out on top, with about an 80 percent return rate. In Asia, the top countries in this respect were Thailand and India (40 percent), Indonesia (35 percent), followed by
40　Malaysia and China (about 20 percent).

4 Encouraged by the results, the researchers tried to get a broader view to see what would happen if the sum of money were larger. This time the amount of money in some of the wallets was higher—the equivalent of around $94, or seven times the amount in the previous experiment. Reporting rates increased from 46
45　percent for wallets without money to 61 percent for wallets containing money and topped out at 72 percent for wallets with the larger sum of money.

5 These results show that not only is a wallet containing money more likely to be returned, but the more money it contains, the more likely it is that this will happen. When attempting to explain the altruistic nature of the findings, the
50　researchers suggested that it was connected to people's self-image. One researcher mentioned that if people commit a dishonest act, they feel a "psychological cost." That is to say, people would rather see themselves as honest than as thieves.

6 One interesting point about these experiments is that they did not include Japan, which has a global reputation for the honesty of its citizens. According
55　to statistics issued by Japan's Metropolitan Police Department*, about 3.5 billion yen in lost cash is handed in to the police every year, whereas about 8.4 billion yen is reported as lost. In other words, the police receive about 40 percent of all the cash reported as lost. Does this mean that Japan's reputation for honesty is justified when these figures are compared with the international research results
60　above? We cannot make an exact comparison, because the statistics given for Japan focus on the amount of cash involved rather than the number of wallets. However, we could note that the experiment examined the honesty of employees of public institutions. People may behave more honestly in their official capacity as* staff members. Japanese statistics, on the other hand, refer to the amount of
65　cash handed over to the police by citizens, not employees. Japanese people may feel an obligation to behave honestly even in their capacity as private citizens. This, rather than the results of an elaborate experiment, strongly suggests that the Japanese deserve their reputation for honesty.

NOTES

Metropolitan Police Department 警視庁（日本の東京都を管轄する警察組織，及び本部。），**in an official capacity as~** ～としての公的な立場で

Choose T if the statement is true or F if it is false.

1. The experiment in paragraph 2 tried to make an international comparison of the general public's honesty. [T] [F]
2. According to the results of the first studies, some Latin American countries did not fit the overall pattern. [T] [F]
3. In the second study, more people emailed to return the wallets with the larger amount of cash. [T] [F]
4. The researchers concluded that people tend to avoid being perceived as dishonest. [T] [F]
5. The author directly compared the results of the international studies with Japan's Metropolitan Police Department statistics to figure out whether Japanese people are more honest than those in other countries. [T] [F]

The figure below shows the differences and the similarities in the data collection procedure between the international studies and Metropolitan Police Department statistics as described in the passage. Choose the differences for blank (1) to (4) and similarities for blank (5) from the list below.

International Studies

- Researchers (1).
- Researchers (2) and ask them to take care of it.

- The police or the owner (5).

Metropolitan Police Department Statistics

- People (3).
- Lost money and wallets are handed over directly to the police (4).

(a) find money or wallets

(b) receive money or wallets

(c) pose as ordinary people who found a wallet

(d) hand the wallet to a staff member in a public institution

(e) by the actual finders

(1) _____ (2) _____ (3) _____ (4) _____ (5) _____

Ⅳ Writing

Organization 2 （Comparison & Contrast）

　文章構成の1つに比較・対照型があります。これは2つのものの特徴を類似点でまとめる「比較」と、相違点でまとめる「対照」で構成されます。書く前に右のような「ベン図」（**Venn diagram**）で類似点と相違点を整理することが有効です。また実際にパラグラフを書くときは、比較・対照のシグナルワードを使うと、分かりやすい英文になります。

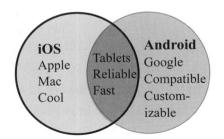

iOS
Apple
Mac
Cool

Tablets
Reliable
Fast

Android
Google
Compatible
Customizable

シグナルワード
比較：be similar to, be the same as, be compared to/with, both A and B, Likewise, Similarly
対照：be different from, be unlike, but, while, whereas, however, in contrast, on the other hand

Exercise

Put the words and phrases in right order.

(1) 世界には1京*匹の蟻がいると推定され、全人類とおおよそ同じ重さがある。
　　*1兆の一万倍
There are an estimated ten thousand trillion ants worldwide, and (as, same, all, the, they weigh, roughly, humanity, of).

....

(2) 言語学習は急な学習カーブを描くため、他の種類の学習とは全く異なる。
(very, other, language learning, is, all, of, from, types, study, different) because it has a steep learning curve.

....

Compare the differences and the similarities in data collection procedure between the international study and Metropolitan Police Department statistics. Write down these points in one paragraph. You can use the words and phrases you learned in the passage or comprehension questions.

....

....

....

....

Listening & Conversation

 1-42

Listen to the dialogue and fill in the blanks. Then, practice the dialogue with your partner.

A: I (¹.   ) my wallet yesterday, but fortunately someone
(².   ) it up and took it to the police.

B: Was the money returned, too?

A: Yes. An honest person returned it, fortunately.

B: Every year, the Metropolitan Police Department publishes (³.   )
data on lost items. Wallets rank fourth overall on the list of lost items.

A: Were they returned to their owners?

B: (⁴.   ) to the data, 64% of lost wallets got back to their owners.

A: Does it mean the other 36% of wallets were not returned to their owners? Why
didn't the owners go to the police?

B: I didn't understand it, (⁵.   ). It sounds very strange.

Discussion

Table 1 shows the number of items lost in Tokyo in a single year. Tables 2 and 3 show how many were returned to their owners and how many were officially disposed of. Compare the data and discuss the differences with your partner.

•Table 1.

Rank	Items	Number of items
1	certificates and official documents	772,301
2	marketable securities	553,741
3	clothes and shoes	494,931
4	wallets	371,789
5	umbrellas	318,601
6	electronics	187,649
7	bags	180,595
8	cell phones	152,972
9	jewelry	114,127
10	cameras and glasses	94,225

•Table 2.

Rank	Items	Returned
1	cell phones	82.5%
2	certificates and official documents	72.1%
3	wallets	64.7%
4	marketable securities	29.6%
5	bags	29.2%
6	electronics	8.2%
7	cameras and glasses	4.8%
8	clothes and shoes	3.8%
9	jewelry	1.6%
10	umbrellas	1.0%

•Table 3.

Rank	Items	Disposed
1	marketable securities	28.9%
2	certificates and official documents	27.7%
3	cell phones	17.5%
4	electronics	7.6%
5	umbrellas	6.0%
6	clothes and shoes	1.5%
7	bags	0.4%
8	cameras and glasses	0.1%
9	wallets	0.0%
10	jewelry	0.0%

UNIT 7

I Am a Cyborg: How Machines Are Meshing with Humans

人間と機械が融合する日

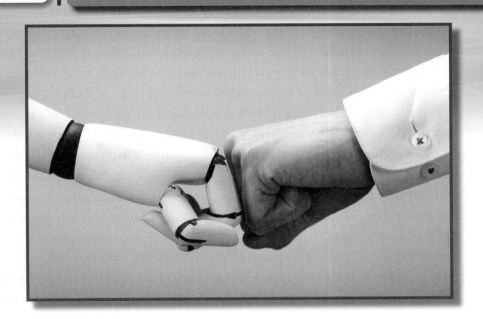

I Warm up

Surprisingly, not a few people in the world have had machines or technological devices surgically implanted in their body. Can you imagine what they are? Share your ideas with your partner.

II Vocabulary

Match each word or phrase with its meaning.

1. artificial _____
2. status _____
3. replacement _____
4. perception _____
5. inevitable _____
6. substantial _____
7. modification _____
8. burdensome _____
9. negate _____
10. be willing to _____

a. 避けられない　　b. 面倒な　　c. 改良　　d. 地位　　e. 知覚　　f. 人工の
g. 〜することに抵抗がない　　h. 代替品　　i. 相当な　　j. 否定する

Read the passage and answer the questions.

1 "I think that the biggest change this century will be that we will stop using technology as a tool and start using technology as part of the body." These are the words of Neil Harbisson, the first person in the world to be officially recognized as a cyborg—in other words, a living being with both natural and artificial parts.

5 **2** He owes his cyborg status to a wearable device that he calls an "eyeborg." This is an antenna that is mounted to his head and attached to a chip implanted in the bone at the back of his skull. Born with a rare form of extreme colorblindness, Harbisson can perceive the world only in different shades of gray. Using the eyeborg, however, he is finally able to perceive color. It functions by analyzing

10 the wavelengths of colors and turning them into sounds, which are then relayed through his bones to his inner ear. This may sound like a replacement for color perception, but in many ways, the eyeborg exceeds human perception. For example, the device is capable of distinguishing 360 different colors, and allows Harbisson to perceive the presence of ultraviolet, which is a non-visible

15 wavelength of light. Given the rapid technological advances we are making, Harbisson believes that it is inevitable that more and more people will start using technology as part of their body.

3 One country where this trend is becoming more widespread is Sweden, where thousands of people have already had microchips inserted underneath

20 their skin. The main purpose of these microchips—usually inserted between the thumb and the index finger—is to make daily life more convenient. For example, they

25 can be used as contactless credit cards, key cards, and transportation passes. Several Swedish companies are offering microchip implants to their employees to help them

30 quickly enter buildings, open

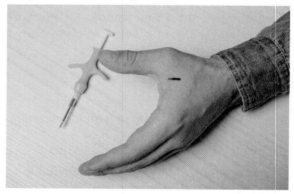

Figure. Microchip implant.

security doors, operate printers, or pay for cafeteria food. Once the chip is embedded beneath your skin, there is no longer any need to worry about misplacing an ID card or carrying a heavy wallet.

4 Various reasons have been suggested to explain why Swedes in particular are

35 more willing to use implanted technology than people in other countries. One is that Sweden is a country where people have a strong belief in the positive

potential of digital technology. Since the government has made substantial investments in technological infrastructure, the Swedish economy is now largely based on digital exports, digital services, and digital tech innovations. As a result,
40 it is one of the world's most successful creators and exporters of digital products and is home to globally successful companies in the digital realm, such as Skype and Spotify.

5 Perhaps a deeper reason is the popularity of the so-called transhumanist movement in Sweden. "Transhumanism" is a belief that we humans should try to
45 escape our biological limitations and upgrade our bodies through incorporating technological devices into them. Winter Mraz, from the U.K., is one example of a growing number of transhumanists. She has microchips in both hands to open doors and send information, as well as LED lights in her arm and five magnets in her left-hand fingers. However, her first cyber-enhancements were not voluntary.
50 She was in a serious car crash that fractured her back, both her ankles, and her knees. After surgery, one of her kneecaps was replaced with a 3D-printed one. If it were not for the cybernetic kneecap, she would not be able to walk. After that experience, she moved on to voluntary personal modifications.

6 It is clear that the idea of incorporating technology into the human body
55 can be viewed in various ways. Swedes, for example, see it as a way to make daily life more convenient and less burdensome. People like Neil Harbisson and some transhumanists see it as a way to expand human perception and abilities. Others, however, may see our willingness to accept technological modification as something that negates our basic identity as human beings. At least, the addition
60 of new abilities modifies our understanding of what it is to be human.

Comprehension Questions A

Choose T if the statement is true or F if it is false.

1. Neil Harbisson implanted eyeborgs in his eyes because he was born with a rare form of colorblindness.   T F

2. Several companies in Sweden require their employees to implant microchips so that they can access their workplace and comply with security systems.   T F

3. A belief in the positive potential of digital technology has strongly affected acceptance of implanted technology in Sweden.   T F

4. Transhumanism refers to the belief that humans can evolve beyond their natural capabilities, especially by means of science and technology.   T F

5. Most of the devices in Winter Mraz's body are intended to be used for medical purposes.   T F

The figure below shows the causes and effects related to the ideas Swedes have about implanted technology as described in the passage. Choose the best answer to fill in the blanks.

Causes (or Reasons)

• Swedish people have a strong trust in digital technology's (1.).

• Many Swedish people are in favor of transhumanism in which (2.) of human body parts with (3.) ones is considered to be a virtue.

• Many people in Sweden have (4.) microchips under their skin so that they can have (5.) access to public transportation, can avoid (6.) payment processes, and no (7.) need to worry about missing key cards.

Effects (or Results)

(1) _____ (2) _____ (3) _____ (4) _____

(5) _____ (6) _____ (7) _____

a) longer   b) replacement   c) implanted   d) replace   e) burdensome

f) contactless   g) artificial   h) potential

Ⅳ Writing

Organization 3 （Cause & Effect）

　「因果関係」（**cause & effect**）型の文章構成は、物事の「原因」（**cause** または **reason**）とその「結果」（**effect** または **result**）を説明するためによく用いられます。また、同じ事象に対して、原因の側から結果を説明することも、逆に結果の側から原因を説明することもできるため、それぞれのシグナルワードを理解しておくことが大切です。

シグナルワード

原因：the cause of, the reason is, because of, because/since/as, as a result of, as a consequence of, result in, due to

結果：the first effect of, as a result, as a consequence, consequently, therefore, thus, result in, lead to, cause, have an effect on, affect

● Exercise

Put the words and phrases in right order.

(1) 綿密な議論の結果、私たちはその新しい方法を採用することに決めた。
(discussion, result, as, a, of, the in-depth), we decided to adopt the new method.

....

(2) 近隣地域の急激な人口増加は、慢性的な渋滞を引き起こした。
The rapid population growth in (neighborhood, to, chronic, has, congestion, our, led).

....

Rewrite paragraph 4 of the passage using cause-and-effect signal words from the list above. You can use the words and phrases you learned in the passage or comprehension questions but paraphrase them as necessary.

....

....

....

....

Active Learning

Listening & Conversation

 1-49

Listen to the dialogue and fill in the blanks. Then, practice the dialogue with your partner.

A: I was really surprised to know that thousands of Swedes have implanted microchips just for their (1.   ).

B: I have the same opinion. In Japan, most domestic dogs have microchips in their skin, but not humans.

A: Pet microchips provide (2.   ) ID for pets, don't they?

B: That's right. But I think Neil Harbisson's eyeborg is socially acceptable, because he has congenital colorblindness.

A: But his device is not just a (3.   ) but a kind of human enhancement.

B: Yes, you have a point.

A: The addition of new abilities is controversial, because it (4.   ) our understanding of what is human.

B: We need some forms of (5.   ) standards.

Discussion

Some people have implanted devices for medical purposes, and others have done it for the sake of convenience. How much tolerance should society have for artificially enhancing the body? Discuss your ideas with your partner.

....

....

....

....

....

....

....

....

....

....

....

UNIT 8

Wireless Power Revolution: Smart Pills and Wireless Power Transmission

ワイヤレス充電から電線不要の電柱まで：電力技術の革新

I Warm up

What is wireless technology? Think of some devices that use wireless technology and share your ideas with your partner.

II Vocabulary

Match each word or phrase with its meaning.

1. massive _____
2. power _____
3. transmit _____
4. conventional _____
5. revolutionize _____
6. infrastructure _____
7. viable _____
8. alternative _____
9. take advantage of _____
10. far from _____

---

a. 大改革する　　b. 電力を供給する　　c. 従来の　　d. 巨大な　　e. 代案　　f. 実行可能な

g. ～を巧みに利用する　　h. 伝える　　i. インフラ・設備　　j. ～からほど遠い

Read the passage and answer the questions.

1 Wireless technology is a well-established feature of our daily lives. We take advantage of its power every day through applications such as cellphones, computer networks, Bluetooth connectivity, GPS devices, or satellite TV. Beyond these familiar uses, however researchers are looking for new ways to utilize its
5 potential.

2 Researchers in a hospital in the United States are aiming to use radio waves* to power devices that have been implanted deep within the human body. The technique has been tested on animals and shows that these waves can send power to devices located up to 10 centimeters deep in body tissue from a distance of one
10 meter. However, radio waves tend to dissipate* as they pass through the body and are therefore not strong enough to supply the necessary power. To overcome the problem, the researchers devised a system called "In Vivo Networking" (IVN). An advantage of this system is that the power is transmitted over a wide area.

3 IVN has the potential to open up completely new types of medical applications.
15 Most conventional implanted devices need to reserve space for a battery, which increases the size. This is a problem because larger devices are more likely to trigger a rejection reaction from our bodies. However, devices powered in this way do not need a battery and so they can be made much smaller than conventional implanted devices. In their study, the researchers were working with a prototype
20 that was about the same size as a grain of rice. The technology could be applied to monitoring blood pressure, glucose*, the gut microbiome*, and stomach conditions inside the body and send the information to the outside world. In the brain it could help to stimulate or inhibit neural activity to treat a disease like Parkinson's*. The device could even be installed in an ingestible capsule device,
25 called a "smart pill." Once this pill enters a patient's stomach, radio waves could be used to trigger it to release controlled amounts of a drug at set times.

4 Another application of wireless technology aims to revolutionize the way electric power is distributed*. Conventionally, power grids* use metal cables, but this is far from ideal. For one thing, it is both difficult and costly to extend this
30 kind of power infrastructure into areas that are remote or have difficult terrain*. For another, the power supply can be knocked out for extended periods if cables are damaged, as frequently happens as a result of wildfires, typhoons, or earthquakes.

5 In New Zealand, a private company, Emrod, is looking into setting up a new wireless electric power distribution system. It uses an invisible beam to distribute
35 electricity wirelessly. Greg Kushnir, Emrod's CEO, has pointed out that distribution methods have hardly changed in around 150 years. This system will become a

commercially viable alternative to traditional wire distribution systems.

6 The idea behind the system is quite simple. A transmitting antenna converts energy into electromagnetic radiation*. The system then focuses it into a tight*, 40 cylindrical* beam. The beam is picked up by a receiving antenna. The laboratory prototype currently operates indoors at a distance of two meters. The company plans to conduct a test outdoors very soon.

7 As far as practical applications go, the company is considering the possibility of using the technology to deliver electricity from the southern tip of New Zealand 45 to an island 30 kilometers away. It estimates that the cost could be around 60 percent of that of an undersea cable.

8 Given our increasing familiarity with the power and ease of use of wireless technology in daily life, innovations such as these are beginning to seem less like science fiction and more like "science fact."

NOTES ....

radio wave 電波, **dissipate** 消える, **glucose** グルコース, **gut microbiome** 腸内フローラ, **Parkinson's** パーキンソン病, **distribute** （電力を）送る・送電する, **power grid** 送電網, **terrain** 地形, **electromagnetic radiation** 電磁放射線, **tight** 圧縮された, **cylindrical** 円柱状の

Comprehension Questions A

Choose T if the statement is true or F if it is false.

1. Implanted devices with IVN have highly miniaturized batteries because radio waves send power constantly from outside the body. ☐T ☐F

2. A smart pill is an ingestible capsule that can release medications and stimulate nerve cells in the brain. ☐T ☐F

3. The current method of electricity distribution is vulnerable because the power grid relies on metal cables to carry electricity. ☐T ☐F

4. The new electricity distribution system uses an invisible beam to eliminate traditional metal cables. ☐T ☐F

5. A wireless electric power distribution system has already been commercially used in New Zealand. ☐T ☐F

The figure below shows problems and a solution related to a new way of distributing electric power in New Zealand as described in the passage. Choose the best answer to fill in the blanks.

Problems

- It is too (1.) and too difficult to install (2.) power infrastructure in remote areas or in complicated terrain.
- The (2.) power supply cables are vulnerable because they are often damaged by (3.).

- An (4.) and (5.) system that takes advantage of (6.) electric power distribution was invented by Emrod.

Solution

(1) _____ (2) _____ (3) _____ (4) _____ (5) _____ (6) _____

a) frequency   b) conventional   c) alternative   d) expensive
e) viable   f) wireless   g) natural disasters

Ⅳ　Writing

Organization 4 （Problem & Solution part 1）

　「問題解決」（**problem & solution**）型の文章は、具体的な問題提起とその解決策を提示するためのもので、新たな提案を行ったりする際、読み手を説得するためによく用いられる文章構成です。また、TOEFL や IELTS といった試験のライティング課題でも出題されることが多いため、この文章構成に慣れておくことは有用です。問題解決型の文章には以下の構成要素が含まれることが理想的です。本 Unit ではその基礎的な内容［以下の（1）〜（3）の要素］を扱い、次の Unit でより発展的な内容［以下の（4）あるいは（5）の要素も含む］を扱います。

問題解決型文章の主要構成要素
（**1**）問題点を明示する
（**2**）その問題が解決されるべきものであると読み手に納得させる
（**3**）解決策を提示する
（4）解決策の評価（なぜそれが優れたものであるかの説明）を行う
（5）想定される反論への対策を講じる

シグナルワード
problem, solution, be (re)solved, to solve the problem(s), because, since, as a result, in order to, lead to, result in, cause, so that, far from ideal

Exercise

Put the words in right order.

(1) 地球温暖化が様々な問題を引き起こしつつあることを多くの人が認識している。
Many people are aware that (of, problems, a, is, warming, causing, lot, global).

....

(2) その突発的な問題は、ある科学者の機転によって解決された。
That sudden (by, thinking, solved, quick, the, problem, was, of) a scientist.

....

Explain the problems of conventional power transmission and solution(s) in one paragraph. You can use the words and phrases you learned in the passage or comprehension questions.

....

....

....

 2-09

Listen to the dialogue and fill in the blanks. Then, practice the dialogue with your partner.

A: Do you know about Emrod's long-range wireless power transmission technology?

B: I have never heard of it.

A: It sends electricity over long distances in an (1.   ) beam.

B: Wow! It must (2.   ) the way electric power is distributed.

A: That's right. We don't need electricity cables any more.

B: The installation and (3.   ) of cables is extremely expensive.

A: Yes. Especially (4.   ) islands rely on underwater cables.

B: It's not hard to imagine that underwater cables need expensive
   (5.   ) upgrades.

Discussion

If a wireless electric power transmission system operated in Japan, how would our life change? Discuss your ideas with your partner.

....

....

....

....

....

....

....

....

....

....

....

....

....

The Simple, Free Solution to Myopia? Just Go Outside!

外で遊ぶだけで近視予防？

I Warm up

What is the cause of myopia? Share your ideas with your partner.

II Vocabulary

Match each word or phrase with its meaning.

1. myopia _____
2. vision _____
3. contend _____
4. incidence _____
5. underway _____
6. initiative _____
7. institute _____
8. precisely _____
9. odds _____
10. be prone to _____

a. 視力　　b. 確率　　c. 主張する　　d. ～する傾向がある　　e. 正確に
f. 新たな取り組み　　g. 近視　　h. 発症　　i. 始める　　j. 進行中で

III Reading Comprehension

Read the passage and answer the questions.

1 Myopia, or near-sightedness, is a condition in which objects nearby appear clearly but those farther away look blurry. In recent years, rates of myopia have been on the increase around the world but are particularly high in East Asia. In Japan, a recent study showed that myopia was prevalent in 76.5 percent of
5 children aged six to 11 and in 94.9 percent of those aged 12 to 14. In other words, 19 out of every 20 teenagers in Japan are myopic

2 Myopia may seem to be just a minor problem that can be corrected with glasses, contact lenses, and possibly even laser surgery. The worrying thing, though, is the fact that so many young people are now affected. By the time
10 these people reach their 60s, they may experience much worse problems with their vision. As people age, they run a greater risk of more serious eye disorders such as glaucoma*, cataracts*, and retinal detachment*, all of which could lead to impaired vision and even blindness. It is therefore important to find a way to mitigate the problem.

15 **3** The conventional explanation for the many cases of myopia among younger people is that they spend too much time on so-called "close work" such as studying or staring at smartphones and computer screens. But now the focus is changing. Researchers are proposing that a simple change in lifestyle can have a beneficial effect. They contend that the incidence of myopia can be greatly
20 reduced by having children spend more time outside. An Australian study looked at 4,000 children in Sydney. It established clearly that myopia was less prevalent in children who spent more time out of doors and less time on close work. The reverse was also true: children who spent less time outdoors and did more close work were more prone to myopia. The cause, researchers say, is exposure to
25 sunlight. Children and teenagers need sunlight during the critical years when their eyeballs are still developing. Thus, in addition to doing work that involves focusing on close objects, greater time spent indoors could also be a risk factor for myopia.

4 The problem is how to balance time spent outside with time spent on studying.
30 Experiments are underway to help students get more exposure to sunlight without having their education disrupted. One such initiative is the "Bright Classroom." As an example, there is an elementary school in Guangdong, China, where the school's walls and ceilings are made of transparent plastic, which allows natural light to come through. Even if results from such schools are good, constructing
35 a large number of them would be costly. A lower-cost solution has been tried in Taiwan. In one study, students were locked out of their classrooms during recess

and lunch break. This meant the children got 80 more minutes in sunlight than they had before, and
40 fewer of them developed myopia compared with those from another school that did not institute this policy.

5 At present, the researchers still
45 don't understand precisely what mechanism is at work. One theory suggests that sunlight triggers the release of dopamine in the retina. According to another, it is the blue
50 light from the sun that protects against myopia. This solution, while appearing straightforward on the surface, is not as simple as it appears. The suggestion that children should use their computers or tablets outside seems to do nothing to solve the problem since close work still increases the odds of having myopia. Also, balancing time spent outside with time spent on studying is particularly hard
55 to achieve in some Asian countries, where education is intensely competitive and there is strong social pressure to study hard and pass exams.

Figure. External structure
of the Bright Classroom.

NOTES ....

glaucoma 緑内障, **cataract** 白内障, **retinal detachment** 網膜剥離

Comprehension Questions A

Choose T if the statement is true or F if it is false.

1. The prevalence of myopia seems to be increasing worldwide and to be particularly severe among younger people in Japan. ☐T ☐F

2. People seem to underestimate the possibility that myopia can lead to serious, vision-threatening complications including blindness. ☐T ☐F

3. One of the main causes of myopia is too much exposure to sunlight. ☐T ☐F

4. According to the study in paragraph 4, some students in Taiwan are forced to stay in their classrooms during recess and lunch break. ☐T ☐F

5. Paragraph 5 suggested that reading books outside is one effective way to prevent myopia. ☐T ☐F

The figure below shows a problem and solutions regarding prevention of myopia as described in the passage. Choose the best answer to fill in the blanks.

Problem

- How to (1) time spent outside with time spent on studying.

- Researchers built the "Bright Classroom" that allows (2) in through walls and ceilings made of (3) plastic to test whether high daylight levels indoors can prevent (4).

- In Taiwan, a study asked teachers to lock kids (5) during lunch, forcing them to (6) that time outdoors.

Solutions

(1) _____   (2) _____   (3) _____

(4) _____   (5) _____   (6) _____

a) institute   b) outside   c) sunlight   d) spend   e) transparent

f) myopia   g) balance

Ⅳ Writing

Organization 5 （Problem & Solution part 2）

　Unit 8 で説明したとおり、「問題解決」（**problem & solution**）型の文章では具体的な問題提起とその解決策を提示します。読み手の納得を高めるために、以下に示した（4）解決策の「評価」（evaluation）や（5）想定される反論への対策（＝再反論や反駁；refutation）の要素を結論の中で示すと効果的です。

問題解決型文章の主要構成要素
（1）問題点を明示する
（2）その問題が解決されるべきものであると読み手に納得させる
（3）解決策を提示する
（4）**解決策の評価（なぜそれが優れたものであるかの説明）を行う**
（5）**想定される反論への対策を講じる**

解決策の評価や反駁の表現例
This solution can be implemented easily…
This method is effective to solve the problem…
This is one of the most cost-effective solutions…
This way is practical and feasible…

Exercise

Put the words in right order.

(1) 想定される解決策の中で、私たちの方法が最も実施しやすく、費用対効果の高い方法だと考えています。
Of the possible solutions, we believe that (is, our, implement, to, easiest, method, the) and most cost-effective.

....

(2) あなたが提案した解決策は、効果的に見えますが、実行可能性が低いと指摘せざるを得ません。
We have to point out that the solution you have proposed (effective, but, not, feasible, seems, is).

....

Write your solution(s) to myopia in one paragraph including the evaluation of it/them and/or refutation of some possible objections to it/them. You can use the words and phrases you learned in the passage or comprehension questions.

....
....
....

Listening & Conversation

 2-15

Listen to the dialogue and fill in the blanks. Then, practice the dialogue with your partner.

A: Did you know that a high level of outdoor activity is (1.) related with lower odds of developing myopia?

B: Yes, I was really surprised when a doctor told me.

A: I heard that (2.) history of myopia is also an important (3.).

B: Do you mean genetic factors are related to myopia?

A: Yes. Lower amounts of outdoor activity highly (4.) the odds of people becoming myopic especially when they have two myopic parents.

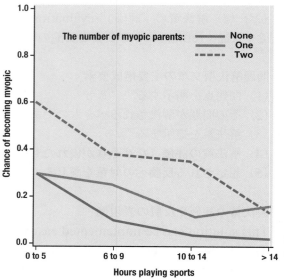

Note. Taken from Jones et al. (2007).

B: In this case, children with no myopic parents and the highest amount of outdoor activity have the (5.) chance of becoming myopic.

A: That's right.

Discussion

How do we balance time spent outside with time spent on studying? Discuss your ideas with your partner.

....

....

....

....

....

....

....

....

UNIT 10

Why Do Zebras Have Stripes?

シマウマはなぜ縞模様？

I Warm up

Do you know why zebras have stripes? Share your ideas with your partner.

II Vocabulary

Match each word or phrase with its meaning.

1. striking _____
2. kingdom _____
3. predator _____
4. dusk _____
5. render _____
6. posit _____
7. eddy _____
8. reiterate _____
9. merge into _____
10. gain momentum _____

a. 界　　b. 夕暮れ　　c. 繰り返し言う　　d. 渦　　e. 人目を引く　　f. 推測する
g. 〜に溶け込む　　h. 〜の状態にする　　i. 勢いを増す　　j. 捕食者

Read the passage and answer the questions.

1 With its black and white-striped markings, the zebra is considered by many to be one of the most visually striking members of the animal kingdom. But beauty alone is not a sufficient explanation for this spectacular feature. Why zebras have stripes is a question that has been discussed as far back as 150 years ago by great
5 Victorian biologists like Charles Darwin.

2 Several explanations have been put forward to explain the zebra's appearance, but a strong scientific consensus has not emerged. One explanation is that stripes serve as camouflage that protects them from predators such as lions. This view may seem counter-intuitive
10 since zebras' markings are so striking. But zebras are at their most vulnerable at dusk, when they gather to drink at water holes. As the
15 daylight fades, the black and white of their stripes merges into a gray color, which renders them more difficult to see. Consequently,
20 it makes it more difficult for predators to hunt them.

Figure 1. Zebras merging into a gray color at dusk.

3 One other explanation is that the stripes serve as individual markers that help the animals to identify each other or to make the best choice of mate. As with human fingerprints, the
25 striping pattern is unique to each individual, yet scientists have found no evidence that zebras can recognize one another by their stripes. In addition, similar non-striped species can differentiate individuals in other ways.

4 Yet another view is that the stripes play a role in thermoregulation. This theory posits that when air strikes a zebra, the currents move more quickly and strongly
30 over the black parts (because black absorbs more heat) than over the white parts. At the points where these two different types of airflow meet, it creates eddies* that serve to cool the zebra down. One scientist claims to have found that heavily striped animals have a body temperature 3 ℃ lower than non-striped animals in the same area.

35 **5** Recently, however, another theory seems to be gaining momentum as the best explanation. This theory holds that the stripes help to protect zebras against

disease-carrying insects. This would be very useful to zebras since the diseases these insects carry are often deadly. Tim Caro, a researcher at the University of California, and his team devised an experiment to observe tabanids* trying to bite
40 zebras. They discovered that tabanids were able to detect the zebra without any problems, but failed to land or decelerate in the terminal stages of their flight. It suggested that tabanids did not see the target, did not regard the striped surface as an appropriate place to land or were confused somehow by the stripe pattern.

6 A team of Japanese researchers
45 cleverly applied zebra research to farming Wagyu cattle. Tomoki Kojima and his research team painted cows with zebra-like striping to see whether it helps
50 to prevent the animals from being bitten by flies. Flies cause cows to graze, eat, and sleep less, and also to bunch together into tightly clumped* groups, which
55 stresses the animals and leads to more injuries. The results showed

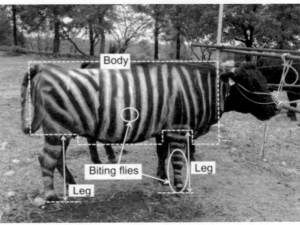

Figure 2. A cow with zebra-like striping.

that painting the cows reduced fly bites by 50 percent. Moreover, zebra-striping reduced fly-repelling behaviors by about 20 percent, indicating that the cows were less bothered by the insects. Researchers believe painting stripes on cattle is a
60 world-first and could become an environmentally friendly alternative to pesticides.

7 In conclusion, it is important to reiterate that the scientific community has not yet universally accepted the theories described above. However, we should bear in mind what evolutionary science tells us: every aspect of a living creature has evolved to give it certain advantages that will help the species survive.

NOTES ....

eddies 渦（**eddy** の複数形），**tabanid** アブ（ハエの一種だが，蚊のように吸血する），**clumped** 群がった

Comprehension Questions A

Choose T if the statement is true or F if it is false.

1. The clearly visible stripes of zebras make them conspicuous under dusk visibility conditions. ☐ T ☐ F
2. One theory suggests that the zebras' stripes serve to distinguish them from other species. ☐ T ☐ F

3. Zebras' stripes are used to help them control their body temperature. ☐T ☐F
4. Tim Caro's research suggests zebras' stripes somehow interfere with the navigational abilities of harmful insects. ☐T ☐F
5. Painting zebra stripes on cattle could be a nature-inspired solution to protect livestock from being bitten by insects. ☐T ☐F

Comprehension Questions B

The figure below summarizes the reasons zebras have stripes. Choose the best phrases or sentence from the list below and fill in the blanks.

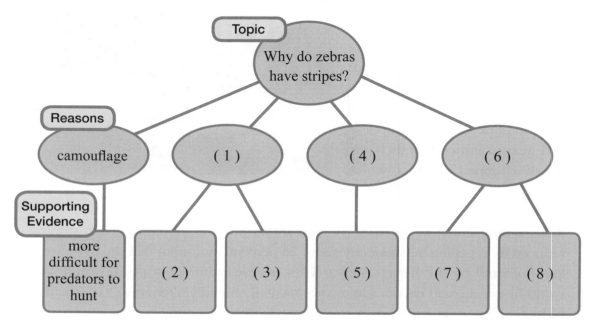

(a) unique to each individual

(b) individual marker

(c) no evidence so far

(d) thermoregulation

(e) protection against disease-carrying insects

(f) Stripes serve to cool zebras.

(g) Stripes interfere with the navigational abilities of insects.

(h) Painting stripes on cattle is an environmentally friendly alternative to pesticides.

(1) _____ (2) _____ (3) _____ (4) _____ (5) _____ (6) _____

(7) _____ (8) _____

Ⅳ Writing

Writing by Purpose 1 (Classification)

Unit 10 〜 Unit 13 では、より発展的な文章構成の方法を学びます。

読解だけでなく、文章を書くときにも情報の仕分け（整理）が重要です。その方法の１つに「概念図」（concept map）があります。概念図とは、情報の構造を階層的に整理する方法です。概念図は、はじめから英語で作成しなくても、以下の例のようにまずは日本語で考えをまとめることも有効です。

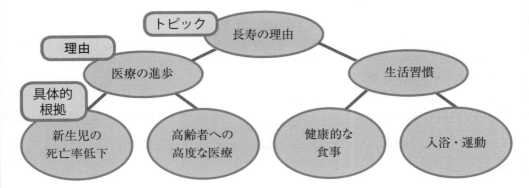

シグナルワード

例示：for example, for instance, take 〜 as an example, because / as / since

理由：because of / due to / on account of / owing to, This is because, in other
　　　words, that is to say

Exercise

Put the words and phrases in right order.

(1) この本は運動不足のために体脂肪の増加リスクがある人にお勧めです。

This book is recommended for a person who is (of, at, of, on, increase, exercise, risk, body fat, account, insufficient).

....

(2) 昇進したければ、例えば、彼は態度を改める必要がある。

For (his, instance, to, corrected, needs, attitude, be) if he wants a promotion.

....

Write down some reasons why zebras have stripes in one paragraph. You can use the words and phrases you learned in the passage or comprehension questions.

....

....

Active Learning

Listening & Conversation

Listen to the dialogue and fill in the blanks. Then, practice the dialogue with your partner.

A: I watched a (1.   ) TV program about wildlife numbers in Kenya.

B: I didn't watch it. How was it?

A: Very interesting. A study team in Nairobi, Kenya, studied wildlife numbers between 1977 and 2016. They (2.   ) 88% of Kenya's land (3.   ).

B: Wow, that was a very large-scale survey!

A: The team showed the numbers of sheep and goats rose 76.3%, and camels 13.1%. But the number of Grevy's zebras fell disastrously. It is an 87% (4.   )!

B: I never knew that zebras are endangered.

A: Not every type of zebra. The plains zebra is not endangered.

B: Plains zebras are very (5.   ), aren't they? I have seen them in a zoo.

Discussion

The following data shows wildlife numbers in Kenya between 1977 and 2016. Some animals increased their numbers, but others didn't. Especially, the number of Grevy's zebras decreased dramatically. Discuss the differences and think about why these differences happened.

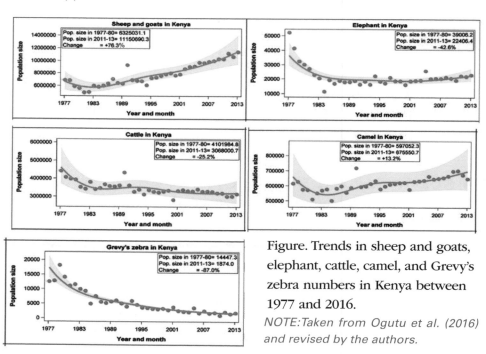

Figure. Trends in sheep and goats, elephant, cattle, camel, and Grevy's zebra numbers in Kenya between 1977 and 2016.

NOTE: Taken from Ogutu et al. (2016) and revised by the authors.

Placebo Effect Is Real: Fake Treatment Do Cure Patient

「病は気から」は本当だった：偽薬で治る人体の不思議

I Warm up

Do you know a medicine that has no therapeutic effect? What purpose is it used for? Share your ideas with your partner.

II Vocabulary

Match each word or phrase with its meaning.

1. pill _____
2. ingredient _____
3. phenomenon _____
4. stimulant _____
5. fatigue _____
6. proportion _____
7. genuine _____
8. advocate _____
9. bring about _____
10. in advance _____

a. 真の   b. ～をもたらす   c. 主張する   d. 疲労   e. 錠剤

f. 刺激   g. 割合   h. 成分   i. 現象   j. 前もって

Read the passage and answer the questions.

1 When a drug manufacturer plans to bring a new product onto the market, it must first conduct extensive tests to determine its safety and effectiveness. One such method involves the use of a placebo*. A placebo is something that appears to be a real medical treatment but is not. For example, it could be a pill or an
5 injection that contains no active medical ingredients and therefore will have no effect. Researchers will typically divide their test subjects into two groups. One of the groups will receive the actual medication while the other group receives a placebo. None of the subjects know which group they have been assigned to. By comparing results from the two groups, the researchers are able to determine
10 whether the drug works or has side effects.

2 This technique is not as straightforward as it may appear owing to a phenomenon known as the "placebo effect." Simply stated, a placebo may bring about effects—either positive or negative—if the patient believes this is what will happen. In one case, people were given a placebo described as a stimulant*, after
15 which their blood pressure rose, and their pulse rate increased. Other people were given the same placebo and told it would help them sleep, which is exactly what happened. Also, if people believe that a placebo will have side effects such as nausea* or headaches, they will often suffer from these symptoms.

3 So, how does the placebo effect work? Essentially, it is a psychobiological
20 phenomenon. One of the most common theories is that the placebo effect is due to a person's expectations of clinical improvement. If someone expects a pill or injection to be effective, such belief could bring about changes in the central nervous system* and cause the improvement. In other words, a patient's belief about a treatment will sometimes trigger physical effects whether or not any
25 active medical ingredient is involved.

4 More surprisingly, placebos can be effective even if patients know in advance that they are taking fake medicine. A recent study at Harvard University in the United States looked at people suffering from irritable bowel syndrome*, a common condition that causes abdominal cramps*, diarrhea*, or constipation*.
30 Half the participants received no medication at all while the other half received what they knew to be a pill that contained no active medication—a so-called "open-label placebo." The results for this latter group showed a dramatic and significant improvement in symptoms. The doctor that headed the research said that even though placebos cannot treat serious conditions such as high cholesterol
35 or cancer, they can help alleviate* various conditions, including pain, nausea, or fatigue.

5 A recent survey conducted in Australia discovered that a substantial proportion of Australian general practitioners reported prescribing a placebo in clinical practice, and 14 percent of them reported prescribing placebos once a month or
40　more. The most cited reason is that they considered placebo treatments as genuine benefits for patients. Despite placebos' lack of medical efficacy, studies show that they actually help patients suffering from pain, nausea, and high blood pressure. The second most frequently stated reason was a patient's expectation or demand for a treatment. It could be that meeting patients' expectations of receiving some
45　kind of treatment will help ease their anxiety, and it is better than giving them nothing at all.

6 Although some doctors around the world are now prescribing placebos to patients, particularly in the United Kingdom, Germany, and Switzerland, the exact mechanisms remain unknown. There needs to be a greater focus on how
50　psychological and social factors can affect physical outcomes. The researchers now advocate further research into how the placebo effect can be harnessed to produce positive results in patient care.

NOTES

placebo プラセボ，偽薬，**stimulant** 興奮剤，**nausea** 吐き気，**central nervous system** 中枢神経系，
irritable bowel syndrome 過敏性腸症候群，**abdominal cramp** 腹部のけいれん，**diarrhea** 下痢，
constipation 便秘，**alleviate** 軽減する

Choose T if the statement is true or F if it is false.

1. Using placebos in clinical trials enables scientists to better understand whether a new medical treatment is safer and more effective than no treatment. ☐T ☐F

2. The placebo effect is beneficial because most people experience improvement. ☐T ☐F

3. The mind can sometimes trick us into believing that a fake treatment has real therapeutic results. ☐T ☐F

4. To obtain a meaningful placebo effect, it is not necessary to deceive patients or conceal information from them. ☐T ☐F

5. A considerable number of doctors in Australia have offered placebos because they believe there are some real benefits to their patients. ☐T ☐F

The table below shows the definitions of words related to "placebo." Choose the best answer to fill in the blanks.

Word(s)	Definition
placebo	A substance that gives no therapeutic (1.) to a patient. It is used to (2.) whether the drug works or has side effects.
placebo effect	A (3.) in which a placebo, an inactive substance like sugar, (4.) or impairs a patient's health condition in accordance with the patient's (5.).
open-label placebo	Pills or injection explained to patients in (6.) containing no active (7.) ingredients.

(1) _____ (2) _____ (3) _____ (4) _____

(5) _____ (6) _____ (7) _____

a) improves   b) improvement   c) determine   d) effect   e) medical

f) advance   g) phenomenon   h) belief   i) believe

Ⅳ Writing

Writing by Purpose 2 （Definition）

　専門的な用語や一般的ではない用語には、文章中で「定義」（definition）や「例」（example）を与えることが大切です。定義を与える表現には、関係代名詞、" — "（ダッシュ）や " , "（カンマ）があります。そのほか、以下の表現もあります。

定義に用いられる表現
A is defined as B, A is described as B, A refer to B, that is (to say), known as, so-called

Exercise

Put the words in right order.

(1) ハイブリッドカーとは、2つ以上のエネルギー源を持つ一種の自動車である。
(kind, is, defined, hybrid, a, a, car, as, of) vehicle with more than one energy source.

....

(2) 科学とは知識を得るためのシステムである。
Science (system, knowledge, to, a, of, acquiring, refers).

....

Explain the terms placebo, placebo-effect, and open-label placebo in one paragraph with examples. You can use the words and phrases you learned in the passage or comprehension questions.

....
....
....
....

Active Learning

 2-30

Listening & Conversation

Listen to the dialogue and fill in the blanks. Then, practice the dialogue with your partner.

A: Have you ever heard of a placebo?

B: Yes, it is a kind of fake medicine, isn't it?

A: That's right. It doesn't include any active medical (1.   ).

B: I heard that placebos are for medical (2.   ). Are they used in medical
(3.   ) in Japan?

A: Actually, the answer is yes. Japanese researchers conducted a nationwide survey on placebo use by nurses and they found that 86% of nurses have used placebos with their patients.

B: Really? Do doctors know about it?

A: Of course. About 90% of cases are done under the (4.   ) of doctors.

B: I think there must be (5.   ) concerns about it.

Discussion

The table below shows the result of a questionnaire survey on placebo use in Japan. The participants were 352 Japanese nurses who work at hospitals. What can you understand from the data? Discuss your ideas with your partner.

Table. The result of a questionnaire survey on placebo use in Japan.

Do you think placebos are effective?	very effective	3%
	effective	45%
	can't say either	49%
	not effective	3%
	not effective at all	0%
Have you ever used placebo?	yes	86%
	less than 5 times	43%
	from 5 to 10 times	26%
	more than 10 times	31%
	no	14%
For what purposes have you used placebo? (multiple answers)	to ease chronic pain	83%
	to treat insomnia	43%
	others	8%
Do you have ethical concerns about placebo use?	yes	41%
	no	59%
Have you ever used placebos without a doctor's permission?	yes	13%
	no	87%

Note: Taken from Tanaka and Komatsu (2011) and revised by the authors.

UNIT 12

How Smart Are Crows? They Even Enjoy Skiing!

カラスはスキーをして遊ぶ！：カラスの知性の謎

I Warm up

Which animals are considered to be intelligent? Share your ideas with your partner.

II Vocabulary

Match each word or phrase with its meaning.

1. primate _____
2. reveal _____
3. transparent _____
4. opaque _____
5. impulse _____
6. speculate _____
7. deliberately _____
8. refine _____
9. aside from _____
10. become accustomed to _____

a. 霊長類　　b. 改善する　　c. 見せる　　d. 意図的に　　e. 不透明な

f. 透明な　　g. 推測する　　h. 衝動　　i. ～に慣れる　　j. ～に加えて

67

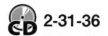
Read the passage and answer the questions.

1 Aside from human beings, chimpanzees and other apes have rightly been considered the most intelligent members of the animal kingdom. However, an increasing body of evidence shows that there is another creature that exhibits equally impressive cognitive skills despite having a much smaller brain—the crow.

2 At one time, it was thought that using tools was a uniquely human skill, but we now know that many other animal species also have this ability. Primates such as chimpanzees employ tools for purposes such as hunting, gathering food and water, shelter, and self-defense. Crows also use tools, but like primates, they do so in a way that reveals high-level cognitive skills. Rather than simply repurposing objects that they find, they can make their own tools. What is more, it has recently been found that crows have an even more advanced skill, previously observed only in humans and primates—the ability to make compound tools.

3 This was discovered through a two-stage experiment. In the first stage, eight crows were presented with a transparent box. Inside was a piece of food, and lying around it were some sticks. The birds soon discovered that they could insert a stick to push the food toward a small opening in the box. The second stage was harder. Instead of sticks, the birds found objects that were too short to be used on their own. But they could be combined to form a tool that was long enough to reach the food. Without any help or previous training, four of the crows figured out how to put the pieces together to form a longer tool and get the food. This impressive achievement took them only 4–6 minutes after first seeing the objects.

4 Another experiment showed that crows share another high-level skill with humans and apes, which is the ability to exercise self-control. In this experiment, the crows first watched a researcher place a piece of food inside an opaque cylinder with openings on each side. The birds soon became accustomed to getting food from these openings. Then the opaque cylinder was replaced by a transparent one with the same openings. Now the crows could see the food inside, but they did not yield to an immediate impulse to get it and hit their head on the plastic material. They remembered what they had learned in the previous test. They walked around to the side of the cylinder and got the food. The results of the cylinder tasks showed that crows performed this task just as well as apes, even though their brains are much smaller. This led researchers to conclude that brain size alone cannot predict the level of an animal's intelligence.

5 Also, like humans, crows love to play. Crows have been observed using tools for what seems like fun. In one famous example, a crow in Russia was filmed using a plastic lid to "ski" down a snowy roof. Scientists speculated that

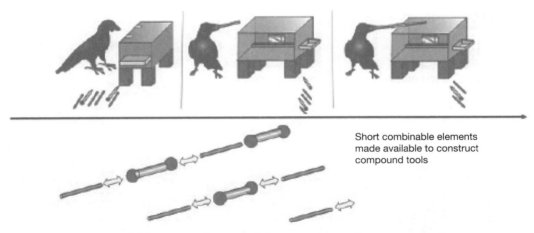

Short combinable elements made available to construct compound tools

Figure. The second stage of the experiment in paragraph 3.

this behavior might be useful in helping the bird understand the concept of slipperiness. Recent research suggests that there is an indirect link between play and the use of tools in crows. In an experiment, some crows were given tools to
40 play with, and these birds were much better at using the tools to find food than birds that did not play with them. There was no evidence, however, that crows deliberately engaged in play as a way to refine their overall problem-solving skills as is the case with human children.

6 Although crows demonstrate an interesting set of behaviors and complex
45 cognitive skills, it does not mean their cognition is necessarily similar to that of humans or apes. Still, it does provide some important insights into the cognitive processes involved in problem solving. The more we learn about what crows are capable of, the more amazing they seem.

Comprehension Questions A

Choose T if the statement is true or F if it is false.

1. Chimpanzees and other apes have more impressive cognitive skills than crows.
   T | F

2. Researchers have discovered that crows can make tools out of multiple parts that are individually useless.
   T | F

3. The research result presented in paragraph 4 showed that the crows' desire for food made them forget what they had already learned.
   T | F

4. Paragraph 5 suggests that playing with objects would help the crows use them to find food in the future.
   T | F

5. Crows play simply because it helps them refine their generalized problem-solving skills.
   T | F

Comprehension Questions B

The chart below shows the procedure and the findings of an experiment to see whether crows have the ability to exercise self-control. Choose the best answer to fill in the blanks in the chart.

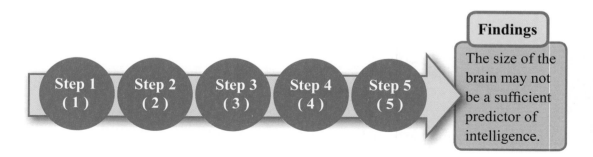

(a) The crows ignore their impulse to directly get the food.

(b) The crows understand that they can eat food from the openings of the cylinder.

(c) Like primates, the crows reveal their potential to accomplish the task.

(d) The crows are aware that the food is inside an opaque cylinder.

(e) The experimenter switches the cylinder out for a transparent one.

Step 1	Step 2	Step 3	Step 4	Step 5

Ⅳ Writing

Writing by Purpose 3 （Procedure & Process part 1）

　スマホの操作方法、料理の作り方、実験の手順、論文の書き方など、何かの「手順」や「手続き」（**procedure**）、「工程」や「過程」（**process**）を説明する機会はたくさんあります。読み手に伝わりやすい文章を書くには、「時系列」（**time order**）や「因果関係」（**cause & effect**）で学んだ知識やシグナルワードが有用です。本 **Unit** では以下のシグナルワードのうち、時系列のシグナルワードを使ってみましょう。

シグナルワード
時系列：first, second, last, next, then, before, after, at the end, in advance, to begin
　　　　with, at the same time, meanwhile, since then

● Exercise

Put the words and phrases in right order.

(1) この機器の安全装置を解除するには、まず裏側のスイッチを押し、その結果、操作可能になる側面の留め具を外す必要がある。

In order to unlock the safety device of this equipment, you first (back, need, to, the, on the, press, switch), and then remove the side clasp that becomes operational.

....

(2) まず、鶏の胸肉を 1/2 インチの小口切りにします。その後、ブドウを 4 分の 1 に切り、セロリ、パセリ、トマトをサイコロ状に切り、ネギをスライスします。

First, (breasts, dice, into, small, up, the chicken) 1/2-inch pieces. Then quarter the grapes, dice the celery, parsley, and tomato, and slice the green onion.

....

Look at the picture in the passage describing how a crow gets a piece of food from a test box. Write down the process in one paragraph using appropriate signal words. You can use the words and phrases you learned in the passage or comprehension questions.

....
....
....
....

Listening & Conversation

 2-37

Listen to the dialogue and fill in the blanks. Then, practice the dialogue with your partner.

A: Do you think crows are clever?

B: Yes! I think they are very (1.   ).

A: I heard that their intelligence can be far more advanced than we thought.

B: Really? But dogs and chimpanzees are more (2.   ) than crows, aren't they?

A: Some people say dogs are as smart as two-year-old children, but recent studies (3.   ) that crows are cleverer than (4.   ) dogs.

B: That's surprising. How did they find out?

A: Researchers had 39 species perform a (5.   ) task. The results showed that 87% of domestic dogs succeeded in completing the task, but 100% of ravens did!

B: That's unbelievable!

Discussion

The table below shows the top 10 performing species in the cylinder task among 39 species. Compare each data and discuss the differences with your partner.

Table. The top 10 performing species in the cylinder task.

Rank	Species	Cylinder task average score	Brain size
1	chimpanzee	100 %	368 m^3
1	raven*（ワタリガラス）	100 %	15 m^3
3	orangutan	99 %	377 m^3
4	jackdaw*（コクマルガラス）	97 %	5 m^3
5	capuchin monkey	96 %	66 m^3
6	bonobo	95 %	341 m^3
6	coyote	95 %	85 m^3
8	gorilla	94 %	490 m^3
9	New Caledonian crow	92 %	7 m^3
10	rhesus monkey	80 %	89 m^3

Note: Taken from Kabadayi, Taylor, von Bayern and Osvath (2016) and revised by the authors.

UNIT 13

Fake Scientific Evidence: Can We Distinguish Science and Pseudoscience?

科学のウソ：ダークチョコレートダイエットの真相

I Warm up

If you were told that chocolate is good for your health, what benefits do you think it would have? Share your ideas with your partner.

II Vocabulary

Match each word or phrase with its meaning.

1. prominently _____
2. feature _____
3. elaborate _____
4. pseudoscience _____
5. assign _____
6. dubious _____
7. rigorously _____
8. enthusiastic _____
9. come up with _____
10. as far as ～ is concerned _____

a. 厳密に　　b. 疑似科学　　c. 怪しげな　　d. 割り当てる　　e. 思いつく
f. 熱狂的な　　g. 目立って　　h. 手の込んだ　　i. 特集する　　j. ～について言えば

III **Reading Comprehension**

 2-38-44

Read the passage and answer the questions.

1 Do you want to lose weight, lower your cholesterol levels, and generally feel better? If so, you should follow the advice of a recent study published in a scientific journal showing that chocolate with high cocoa content can act as a weight-loss accelerator. The claims made by the study were prominently featured
5 in news media in over 20 countries including Japan. You may think these claims sound unbelievable. If you do, then you are correct—the study was part of an elaborate hoax.

2 One of the main figures in this hoax was John Bohannon. Even though he has a Ph.D. in molecular biology, he is a journalist by profession. He was approached
10 by two German TV producers who were working on a documentary film about junk science. At first, they set up a website for the non-existent Institute of Diet and Health, and then added two more key members. One was a doctor, and the other was a statistician. The doctor came up with the idea of testing bitter chocolate as a dietary supplement. When Bohannon asked the reason, the doctor's
15 answer was quite simple but far from scientific: "Bitter chocolate tastes bad. Therefore, it must be good for your health."

3 Next, they recruited a group of 16 test subjects, aged between 19 and 67 to test the weight loss effect of dark chocolate. The subjects were randomly assigned to three groups. One group followed a low-carbohydrate diet. Another followed
20 the same diet along with a small bar of dark chocolate every day. The remaining subjects were used as the control group*.

4 The results showed both of the groups who dieted lost their body weight over the three-week study, but the people in the group that ate chocolate lost weight 10 percent faster, had lower cholesterol readings, and achieved higher scores
25 on a well-being survey*. However, the statistical methods that produced these results was fundamentally flawed. The problem was that there were too many measurements for too few people. As a result, random
30 factors* skewed their conclusions.

5 Bohannon and his colleagues then submitted a paper outlining their results to several dubious journals that were known to
35 publish papers without reviewing them. After receiving several

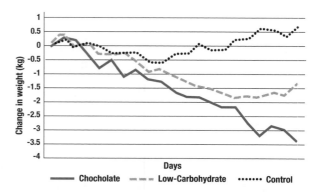

Figure. Daily weight development by group.

positive replies, they finally chose one that agreed to publish their paper for a fee of 600 euros. Though the editor claimed that all the papers published in the journal are rigorously reviewed, the paper appeared with no changes made to the
40 original.

6 The next step was to prepare a press release. As an experienced journalist himself, Bohannon was able to craft it so that it would be immediately appealing to other journalists. The first publication to pick up the story was *Bild*, one of Germany's most popular newspapers. Then, it made headlines in the U.K., Ireland,
45 the U.S., India, Australia, and Japan. This enthusiastic and unquestioning reaction shows how fake nutrition science can easily spread to the world.

7 Bohannon's large-scale trick was completely successful. But, why did the journalist try to deceive the media? His aim was to test health reporters to see whether they could distinguish a dubious science story from a reliable one.
50 Bohannon says that when reporters contacted him, they asked no serious questions about how the study was conducted and ended up publishing the group's findings uncritically. The chocolate diet hoax shows us that even professional journalists and publishers are not always conscientious enough in verifying truth and accuracy. One wider point that comes from this story is how
55 important it is to be cautious about evaluating information. This is especially true as far as social media is concerned, because people are free to post anything they like, and companies like Facebook and Twitter have been criticized for allowing false information to be posted regularly on their platforms.

NOTES ....

control group 統制群（実験処理を行わないグループのこと。ここではダイエットをしないグループを指す。）, **well-being survey** 幸福度調査, **random factor** ランダム要因

Comprehension Questions A

Choose T if the statement is true or F if it is false.

1. Although the weight loss effect of dark chocolate is widely recognized, there has not been much scientific evidence of this claim so far. ☐T ☐F

2. According to paragraph 3, a large number of participants were randomly selected from a wide range of age groups. ☐T ☐F

3. Though Bohannon's research result showed dark chocolate had a weight loss effect, the study was inadequate in its statistical methods. ☐T ☐F

4. The news industry was skeptical about the dietary effect of dark chocolate and reluctant to release the news. ☐ T ☐ F

5. The intention of the people behind the chocolate diet hoax was to raise serious questions about how easily "junk science" can make headlines without being seriously examined. ☐ T ☐ F

Comprehension Questions B

The chart below shows the process of how Bohannon and his team tricked news media into believing dark chocolate has a weight loss effect. Choose the best answer for each blank.

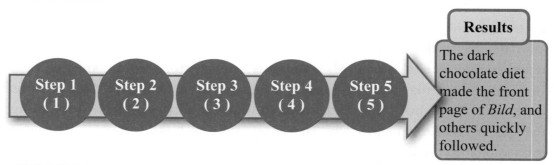

(a) They created a fake (①) called the Institute of Diet and Health and set up a website for it.

(b) From (②) statistical analysis, they irresponsibly stated the weight loss effect of dark chocolate.

(c) They (③) their paper to dubious academic journals.

(d) Bohannon used his media experience to get the results publicized.

(e) They ran a clinical trial with one-third of the subjects randomly put on a low-carb diet, one-third (④) to the same low-carb diet plus eating dark chocolate, and a (⑤) group.

Step 1	Step 2	Step 3	Step 4	Step 5

① _____ ② _____ ③ _____ ④ _____ ⑤ _____

a) assigning   b) assigned   c) control   d) improper   e) organization
f) submitted   g) pseudoscience

Ⅳ　Writing

Writing by Purpose 4 （Procedure & Process part 2）

　Unit 12 では「手順」や「手続き」（**procedure**）／「工程」や「過程」（**process**）を説明する時に「時系列」（**time order**）や「因果関係」（**cause & effect**）で学んだ知識やシグナルワードが有用であることを説明しました。本 **Unit** では因果関係（原因と結果）のシグナルワードを使ってみましょう。

シグナルワード

原因：　the cause of, the reason is, because of, because/since/as, as a result of, as a consequence of, result in, due to

結果：　the first effect of, as a result, as a consequence, consequently, therefore, thus, result in, lead to, cause, have effects on, affect

Exercise

Put the words and phrases in right order.

(1) 今回の衛星放出の成功の第一歩が、次の人工衛星ミッションに繋がることを期待します。

I hope this successful first step in satellite deployment (the next, stage, to, of, lead, satellite, will) missions.

....

(2) この統計解析では、選択された値が 2 番目の検証プロセスに影響を与えます。

In this statistical analysis, the value (on, process, validation, chosen, will, have, an effect, the second).

....

Look at the figure in the passage showing the effects of the diet on participants' weight. Describe the process in one paragraph using appropriate cause-and-effect signal words. You can use the words and phrases you learned in the passage or comprehension questions.

....

....

....

....

Active Learning

Listen to the dialogue and fill in the blanks. Then, practice the dialogue with your partner.

A: I eat dark chocolate every day because I heard it's good for weight loss.

B: Well, I don't think it's a good idea. As (1.   ) as I know, a chocolate diet is an example of (2.   ).

A: Really? But the evening TV news said it has been (3.   ) proved that it can help with weight loss.

B: You're right. The chocolate diet study made headlines around the world, but this was an (4.   ) hoax by an American journalist.

A: A hoax! Unbelievable! Similar things often happen on social media. According to a recent survey on Twitter, false information is 70% more likely to be retweeted and reaches people six times faster than the truth.

B: People like to (5.   ) novel information, so false news is created because it seems more novel and appealing.

Discussion

How do we distinguish false from reliable information? Disuss your ideas with your partner.

....

....

....

....

....

....

....

....

....

....

....

....

....

UNIT 14

Pizza, Milk and Nursing Food: All 3D-Printed

ピザ、ミルクや介護食を **3D** プリンタで " 出力 "

I Warm up

Do you know about 3D printers? What kinds of things can a 3D printer make? Share your ideas with your partner.

II Vocabulary

Match each word or phrase with its meaning.

1. fashion _____
2. blueprint _____
3. consistently _____
4. protein _____
5. swallow _____
6. commercially _____
7. address _____
8. resident _____
9. a wide range of _____
10. by means of _____

---

a. 商業的に　　b. ～を用いて　　c. 作り出す　　d. 扱う　　e. 飲み込む

f. 一貫して　　g. 居住者　　h. 幅広い　　i. たんぱく質　　j. 設計図

Read the passage and answer the questions.

1 The concept of 3D printing has now become familiar enough that we are not surprised to learn that a 3D printer can fashion a huge array of useful and desirable objects such as automobile parts, jewelry, toys, and clothing. But more interestingly, the technology is also making great progress in another area that
5 could have a great impact on our everyday life, and that is 3D-printed food.

2 3D printing now has the capability to produce a wide range of foods. For example, a Silicon Valley company called BeeHex has come up with a device that can produce pizzas. The machine functions by means of cartridges that are loaded with pizza ingredients such as dough, cheese, and tomato sauce. A pressurized
10 system pushes them out through nozzles in the correct proportions. It prints a custom-shaped pizza end-to-end in just one minute. And pizzas no longer have to be circular. The machine can consistently and rapidly make uniquely shaped pizzas, including ones shaped like hearts or even company logos! Customers will be able to order and pay through a smartphone app. They can customize their
15 order and receive a push notification when the food is ready.

3 It is not only pizza production that 3D printing is targeting. Producing animal-free dairy products has also become a goal of some high-tech companies. One such firm is Perfect Day, a company in San Francisco. The company has developed "3D-printed milk." The process itself is quite simple. First, they use a biotech 3D
20 printer to recreate a blueprint of a cow's DNA in a laboratory. They then insert the cow DNA sequence into yeast. When sugar is fed to the special yeast, it produces a huge amount of whey protein, the same proteins in milk that comes from cows. After that, the yeast is removed using filtration, leaving only the proteins that have been created. Finally, the protein is dried into a powder. When it is combined with
25 water, plant-based fats, vitamins, and minerals, in exactly the same proportions as cow's milk, what we get is milk. Recently, Perfect Day did a limited release of three ice cream flavors made with its cow-free milk, and customers said they tasted just like real ice cream.

4 One important area in which 3D food printing can make a difference, is
30 senior care, a growing sector in Japan. People who are aged and infirm often have trouble chewing and swallowing normal food. Nursing food has been commercially produced for this market, but it normally takes the form of a muddy paste, which, while nutritious, is unappetizing. Associate Professor Masaru Kawakami wants to address this problem. He heads a research team that is aiming
35 to use 3D printing to create a nursing food with a texture and appearance similar to regular food. His idea is that by using multiple nozzles on a 3D printer, it is

possible to combine materials
that have a different hardness and
taste to create food that varies
40 in color and texture, thereby
making it more appetizing. He
hopes that in the future, nursing
homes will adopt 3D printers so
that they can produce nursing
45 meals better suited to the tastes
and physical conditions of their
residents.

Figure. The 3D printer making nursing food.

5 These are just a few examples of the great strides being made in 3D printing
technology for food. The new worlds it opens up could help relieve serious
50 problems caused by our current methods of food production such as cost, effects
on human and animal health, and the burden on the environment.

Comprehension Questions A

Choose T if the statement is true or F if it is false.

1. The 3D pizza printing machine can produce pizza in various shapes, but it takes
more time than human chefs. T F

2. To create cow-free protein, a biotech 3D printer is used to print cow DNA sequence
and place it into specific locations in the yeast. T F

3. Perfect Day invented a revolutionary 3D-printing machine which can even print
liquid such as milk. T F

4. Most nursing food is criticized for being unappetizing and low in nutritional value.
T F

5. Associate Professor Masaru Kawakami used a 3D food printer to improve the
quality of elderly people's diets. T F

The following paragraph is a summary of the passage. Choose the best answer to fill in the blanks.

3D printing is now (1.   ) of making food as well as objects. A 3D-printed pizza can be produced in one minute by (2.   ) the material. Another food that can be 3D-printed is milk. 3D-printed milk can be made by printing the DNA (3.   ) of a cow and mixing it with water and other (4.   ) after fermentation. The development of such technology is expected to be (5.   ) to the creation of nursing food that looks and tastes like a regular meal. Thanks to the technological advancement in 3D printers, a variety of contemporary problems related to food production such as high cost and negative (6.   ) on health and the environment could be (7.   ).

(1) _____   (2) _____   (3) _____   (4) _____

(5) _____   (6) _____   (7) _____

a) able   b) sequence   c) applied   d) solved   e) impact   f) capable

g) pressurizing   h) nutrients

Ⅳ　Writing

Writing in Action 1 （Writing a Summary part 1）

　読んだ文章の内容やその要点を「自分の言葉」でまとめること、つまり文章の「要約」（**summary**）は非常に重要なスキルです。本 Unit と Unit 15 で、その方法を説明します。要約は読んだ文章（原文）の長さと要約の長さで情報の圧縮率が変動します。一般的に、圧縮率が高くなるほど、要約作成の難易度は高くなります。本 Unit では**段落単位の要約作成**の練習を行います。

summary の方法
1. 文章全体をよく読み、全体的な内容をしっかり理解する。
2. 文章の主題（Unit 2 参照）や書き手の意見のうち重要なものに下線を引いたり書き出したりする。その際、必要不可欠な情報と省略しても差し支えない情報に仕分けする。
　※省略できる情報の例：書き手が読み手の理解を深めるために補足的に書き加えたと思われる具体例等の情報。
3. 下線を引いたり書き出したりした必要不可欠な情報を再構成する。その際、原文の表現のコピペは厳禁。「自分の言葉」で言い換える（paraphrase する）。
4. できあがった要約の案を読み直し、原文の必要不可欠な情報が漏れていないか、原文に書かれていない情報を勝手に加えていないか、よく確認する。必要に応じて修正を行う。

paraphrase の方法
（ⅰ）従属接続詞が用いられている文を分詞構文を使って言い換える。
（ⅱ）セミコロンやコロンなどの句読法（punctuation）を用いて 2 文を統合させる。
（ⅲ）文の態（能動態 ⇔ 受動態）を替えたり、一文中の語順を入れ替えたりする。
（ⅳ）原文で用いられている語や句に対しての同義語や類語を示すことで言い換える。
（ⅴ）原文で用いられている語や句の品詞を替えて言い換える（word family）。

（山西・大野, 2017）

Summarize paragraph 3 of the passage into 50–60 words. Use the words and phrases you learned in the passage or comprehension questions but paraphrase them as necessary.

Listening & Conversation

 2-51

Listen to the dialogue and fill in the blanks. Then, practice the dialogue with your partner.

A: Advances in 3D-printing technology have been (1.   ). It can make a wide variety of three-dimensional solid objects such as automobile parts, jewelry, toys, and clothing.

B: I agree. Recent 3D printers can even make food such as pizza, pasta, and chocolates.

A: But I wouldn't (2.   ) choose food that had been 3D-printed.

B: I heard 3D-printing food reduces food (3.   ) because it uses only the required amount of raw (4.   ) to make food.

A: I see. So, in other words, it's environmentally friendly.

B: One of the most famous Italian pasta manufacturers, Barilla, is trying to develop a 3D printer (5.   ) of printing beautifully designed pasta, which would be difficult for humans to make.

A: That sounds interesting!

Discussion

Which would you choose, pizza made by a 3D printer or pizza made by humans? Discuss your ideas with your partner.

....

....

....

....

....

....

....

....

....

....

....

....

Science of Lying: Start with Little Lies and then Get Bigger and Bigger

要注意：うそをつくほど「うそつき」になることが判明

I Warm up

Some people believe lying is a necessary social skill. How many times do we lie in a 24-hour period? Share your ideas with your partner.

II Vocabulary

Match each word or phrase with its meaning.

1. occasion _____
2. deliberate _____
3. subject _____
4. capacity _____
5. awkward _____
6. conflict _____
7. immensely _____
8. reinforce _____
9. harmless _____
10. put a burden on _____

a. 被験者　　b. 対立　　c. 容量　　d. 不器用な　　e. 非常に　　f. 場合
g. 意図的な　　h. 〜に負担をかける　　i. 促進する　　j. 無害な

Read the passage and answer the questions.

1 No matter how much we may disapprove of lying, it is impossible to deny that everyone does it sometimes. Sometimes our motive for telling a lie can be understandable. Parents, for example, may tell a so-called "white lie" to their children to protect them from an unpleasant truth. In this case, most people
5 regard lying as an unfortunate but inevitable fact of life. On other occasions, people lie to gain an advantage over others. In the public estimation, some politicians are regarded as notorious liars, who use deliberate untruths to bolster their own power or cover up their bad actions.

2 Fortunately, most people do not regularly tell lies. A study conducted in the
10 United States found that most adults reported not telling any lies in a 24-hour period. Of the lies that were reported, almost half were told by a small group—just 5 percent of the participants—with most people being dishonest only when telling the truth would create problems.

3 Cognitively speaking, it seems that lying puts a greater burden on the brain
15 than telling the truth. A Harvard University scientist conducted an experiment in which he gave participants the chance to deceive others to gain money. While they were making the decision, he used an fMRI* machine to analyze blood flow in their brains. Most participants told the truth automatically. Those that did not exhibited more activity in the brain area that is involved in difficult or complex
20 thinking.

4 A significant study was conducted at Duke University in the United States, led by the well-known neuroscientist Dan Ariely.
25 The researchers found that when people told a lie, there was a burst of activity in their amygdala*. This is a part of the brain responsible for producing emotional responses
30 such as fear and anxiety. However, the really interesting part of the experiment followed. The scientists had the subjects play a game in which they could win
35 money by deceiving their partner. The researchers discovered that

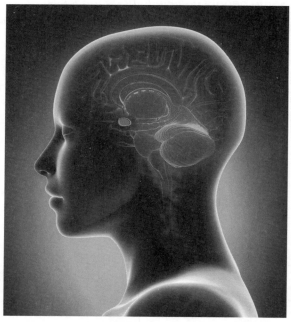

Figure. The Amygdala in the human brain.

during this activity, the negative signals sent by the amygdala began to decrease. What is more, when people discovered that their dishonesty had no negative consequences, their lies became more complex and elaborate. The conclusion
40 seems to be that if we find that lying is successful, we are likely to do it more often. In other words, it creates a feedback loop in which thinking a thought or performing an action makes it easier to do the same thing again in the future.

5 But there is also a bright side to discovering that our brains work this way, which is that telling the truth will increase our capacity for honesty. Our natural
45 tendency is to think that being honest with others will be awkward and cause conflict. However, a recent study conducted at the University of Chicago showed that the opposite is true. People were asked to spend a few days being open and honest, and to think about their expectation of this behavior and its actual results. To their surprise, they discovered that being honest with others is a more pleasant
50 experience and causes much less harm to relationships than they expected.

6 One general truth we can draw from these studies is that our brain is an immensely powerful tool that is not always under our conscious control. We must be aware that we can unconsciously program it in different ways, and so we should be careful to reinforce positive rather than negative behaviors. The act of
55 lying is not harmless—it actually changes us.

NOTES ....

fMRI 脳の活動領域をピンポイントで示すことができる装置, **amygdala** 扁桃（へんとう）体

Comprehension Questions A

Choose T if the statement is true or F if it is false.

1. Notorious liars use elaborate lies for their own benefits as well as to avoid hurting someone's feelings. ☐T☐F

2. The research results presented in paragraph 3 suggested that people struggle with themselves about whether they should tell a lie when they have the opportunity to do so. ☐T☐F

3. The amygdala is a part of the brain that controls key functions relating to communication, memory, and attention. ☐T☐F

4. According to paragraph 4, scientific evidence showed how dishonesty alters people's brain function. ☐T☐F

5. The results of the study mentioned in paragraph 5 suggested that our fears about telling others what we really think are misguided. ☐T☐F

The following paragraph is a summary of the passage. Choose the best answer to fill in the blanks.

People lie for a variety of reasons, but many people lie only when it is truly necessary. And in many cases, lying is (　1.　) demanding, particularly on the amygdala. However, one experiment found that the amygdala's response to lying (　2.　) with every lie. It was also found that if the lies were successful, dishonesty escalated into more complex and (　3.　) lies. On the other hand, other research (　4.　) the consequences of being honest in everyday life suggested that expecting honesty to be less (　5.　) and less socially connected was misguided; honest conversations were far more enjoyable and (　6.　) than they expected. These results suggest that we should be oriented more toward positive behaviors than negative ones.

(1) _____　　(2) _____　　(3) _____　　(4) _____

(5) _____　　(6) _____

---

　　a) decreased　　b) harmless　　c) cognitively　　d) harm　　e) pleasant

　　f) exploring　　g) elaborate　　h) explored

Ⅳ Writing

Writing in Action 2 （Writing a Summary part 2）

　本 Unit では Unit 14 に引き続き文章の「要約」（**summary**），特に文章全体の要約作成を行います。**各段落の要点をつなぎ合わせる際、適切なシグナルワードの使用や効果的な段落の構成が有効です。**これまで学んできたシグナルワードや文章構成をしっかりと活用しましょう。

これまで学んできたシグナルワード
1. 時系列のシグナルワード：first, second, last, next, then, before, after, at the end, in advance, to begin with, at the same time, meanwhile, since then
2. 比較のシグナルワード：be similar to, be the same as, be compared to/with, both A and B, Likewise, Similarly
3. 対照のシグナルワード：be different from, be unlike, but, while, whereas, however, in contrast, on the other hand
4. 原因のシグナルワード：the cause of, the reason is, because of, because/since/as, as a result of, as a consequence of, result in, due to
5. 結果のシグナルワード：the first effect of, as a result, as a consequence, consequently, therefore, thus, result in, lead to, cause, have effects on, affect
6. 問題解決のシグナルワード：problem, solution, be (re)solved, to solve the problem(s), because, since, as a result, in order to, lead to, result in, cause, so that, far from ideal

これまで学んできた文章構成
1. 段落構造→ Unit 1 〜 Unit 4
2. 時系列の文章構成→ Unit 5
3. 比較・対照の文章構成→ Unit 6
4. 因果関係の文章構成→ Unit 7
5. 問題解決の文章構成→ Unit 8・Unit 9

Summarize the whole passage into around 150 words, particularly paying attention to signal words and paragraph organization you have learned. You can use the words and phrases you learned in the passage or comprehension questions but paraphrase them as necessary.

....
....
....
....

Active Learning

Listening & Conversation

Listen to the dialogue and fill in the blanks. Then, practice the dialogue with your partner.

A: Why do you think people tell lies?

B: I'm not sure, but avoiding (1.   ) could be one reason.

A: Yes, it could be. Protecting someone else from (2.   ) is another important reason, I think.

B: That's a good point. It's called a "white lie." Most parents do this to protect their children from an unpleasant truth.

A: White lies are sometimes socially (3.   ). For example, mentioning Santa Claus is acceptable because it protects a child's innocence or creative imagination.

B: I agree. Do you think telling lies is an (4.   ) part of social life?

A: I don't think so. Telling lies could cause (5.   ) with others after a while.

B: Being honest is one of the most important virtues in social life.

Discussion

The figure below shows the frequency and the distribution of reported lying in a 24-hour-period in the adult population of the United States. What can you tell from the data? Discuss your ideas with your partner.

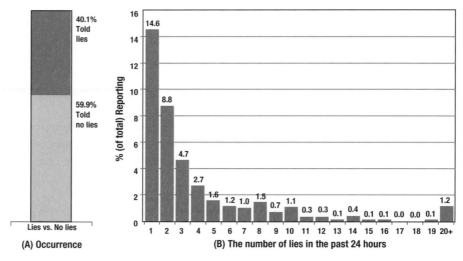

Figure. Occurrence and the number of lies in the past 24 hours.

Note: Taken from Serota, Levine & Bostet (2010).

TEXT PRODUCTION STAFF

| edited by | 編集 |
| Mitsugu Shishido | 宍戸　貢 |

| cover design by | 表紙デザイン |
| Nobuyoshi Fujino | 藤野 伸芳 |

| text design by | 本文デザイン |
| Nobuyoshi Fujino | 藤野 伸芳 |

CD PRODUCTION STAFF

narrated by	吹き込み者
Howard Colefield (AmerE)	ハワード・コルフィールド（アメリカ英語）
Rachel Walzer (AmerE)	レイチェル・ワルザー（アメリカ英語）

Our Science
最新研究から読む世界のおもしろ科学

2023年 1月20日　初版発行
2023年 3月30日　第3刷発行

著　　者　田中 博晃
　　　　　山西 博之
　　　　　Bill Benfield

発 行 者　佐野 英一郎

発 行 所　株式会社 成美堂
　　　　　〒101-0052　東京都千代田区神田小川町3-22
　　　　　TEL 03-3291-2261　FAX 03-3293-5490
　　　　　https://www.seibido.co.jp

印 刷・製 本　倉敷印刷株式会社

ISBN 978-4-7919-7264-7　　　　　　　　　　　Printed in Japan